Visual Arts

as a Way of Knowing

KAROLYNNE GEE

Stenhouse Publishers

The Galef Institute

Strategies for Teaching and Learning Professional Library

Administrators: Supporting School Change by Robert Wortman
Assessment: Continuous Learning by Lois Bridges
Creating Your Classroom Community by Lois Bridges
Dance as a Way of Knowing by Jennifer Zakkai
Drama as a Way of Knowing by Paul G. Heller
Literature as a Way of Knowing by Kathy G. Short
Math as a Way of Knowing by Susan Ohanian
Music as a Way of Knowing by Nick Page
Science as a Way of Knowing by Susan M. Blunck
Second Language Learners by Stephen Cary
Visual Arts as a Way of Knowing by Karolynne Gee
Writing as a Way of Knowing by Lois Bridges

Stenhouse Publishers, 431 York Street, York, Maine 03909
The Galef Institute, 11050 Santa Monica Boulevard, Third Floor, Los Angeles, California 90025

Library of Congress Cataloging-in-Publication Data
Gee, Karolynne.
    Visual Arts as a way of knowing / Karolynne Gee.
      p.   cm. — (Strategies for teaching and learning professional library)
    Includes bibliographical references. (p.   ).
    ISBN 1-57110-090-3
    1. Art—Study and teaching (Elementary)—United States.
    I. Title. II. Title: Visual arts. III. Series.
    N362.G44 1999
    372.5'2044—dc21
                                                                        99-34780
                                                                        CIP

Manufactured in the United States of America on acid-free paper.
03 02 01 00 99 9 8 7 6 5 4 3 2 1

Dear Colleague,

The extraordinary resource books in this series support our common goal as educators to apply best practices to everyday teaching. These books will encourage you to examine new resources and to discover and try out new and different teaching strategies. We hope you'll want to discuss and reflect on your strategies with other teachers and coaches in your support study group meetings (both face-to-face and virtual) to make the most of the rich learning and teaching opportunities each discipline offers.

If we truly believe that all children can be successful in school, then we must find ways to help all children develop to their full potential. This requires an understanding of how children learn, thoughtful preparation of curriculum, continuous reflection, adaptation of everyday practices, and ongoing professional support. To that end, the *Strategies for Teaching and Learning Professional Library* was developed. The series offers you countless opportunities for professional growth. It's rather like having your own workshops, coaching, and study groups between the covers of a book.

Each book in this series invites you to explore
- the theory regarding human learning and development—so you know why,
- the best instructional practices—so you know how, and
- continuous assessment of your students' learning as well as your own teaching and understanding—so you and your students know that you know.

The books offer *Dialogues* to reflect upon your practices, on your own and in study groups. The Dialogues invite responses to self-evaluative questions, and encourage experimentation with new instructional strategies.

Shoptalks provide short, lively reviews of the best and latest professional literature as well as professional journals and associations.

Teacher-To-Teacher Field Notes are full of tips and experiences from other practicing educators who offer different ways of thinking about teaching practices and a wide range of successful, practical classroom strategies and techniques to draw upon.

It's our hope that as you explore and reflect on your teaching practice, you'll continue to expand your teaching repertoire and share your success with your colleagues.

Sincerely,

Linda Johannesen

Linda Johannesen
President
The Galef Institute

The Strategies for Teaching and Learning Professional Library is part of the Galef Institute's school reform initiative *Different Ways of Knowing*.

Different Ways of Knowing is a philosophy of education based on research in child development, cognitive theory, and multiple intelligences. It offers teachers, administrators, artists and other specialists, and other school and district educators continuing professional growth opportunities integrated with teaching and learning materials. The materials are supportive of culturally and linguistically diverse school populations and help all teachers and children to be successful. Teaching strategies focus on interdisciplinary, thematic instruction integrating history and social studies with the performing and visual arts, literature, writing, math, and science. Developed with the leadership of Senior Author Linda Johannesen, *Different Ways of Knowing* has been field tested in hundreds of classrooms across the country.

For more information, contact

The Galef Institute
11050 Santa Monica Boulevard, Third Floor, Los Angeles, California 90025
Tel 310.479.8883
Fax 310.473.9720
www.dwoknet.galef.org

Strategies for Teaching and Learning Professional Library

Contributors	*Editor*	*Designer and Typographer*
President	Resa Gabe Nikol	Delfina Marquez-Noé
Linda Johannesen		
	Editorial Assistants	*Photographers*
Senior Vice President	Shirley Chung	Ted Beauregard
Sue Beauregard	Christine DeBoer	Dana Ross
	Patricia Hynes	

I am grateful to the many children and teachers who have helped me to understand the power of teaching art from the inside–out. That means uncovering the natural artist in every person and nurturing every spark of creativity and imagination. My thanks to teachers for generously sharing their personal reflections about making art as adults and the courage it has provided them for facilitating art activities with their students. Their stories have helped me frame my approach to writing this book.

A special acknowledgment to artist educators and teaching colleagues, Jan Cohn, Pamela Considine, Karen DeJarnette, Faith Dennis, Laurine DiRocco, Jeffrey Dorsey, Hawley Hussey, Alice Mendoza, Delfina Marquez-Noé, Joan Peterson, Catherine Rubin, Yuki Yoshino, and Jennifer Zakkai. They challenged my thinking and caused me to consider new possibilities. And my appreciation to Richard C. Williams for his mentoring and support of collegial learning through the integration of the arts: His vision allowed me to make the connections.

I have had the expert support of the design and editorial staff of the Galef Institue, led by Sue Beauregard , who are in a real sense contributors and co-authors of this book. I thank them wholeheartedly. To my husband, Randy, our daughters Amanda and Pamela, and our grandchildren, Lina, Michel, and Patrick, thank you for merging art and life as a source of personal inspiration and joy.

Special thanks to Andrew G. Galef and Bronya Pereira Galef for their continuing commitment to our nation's children and educators.

Karolynne Gee

Contents

Chapter 1

Art Is Powerful

Art is very, very powerful. It is for everybody in the world. Even some people who don't know how are very good at art in their way.

Alberto, age 10

Art *is* powerful. We marvel at the intricate carving of a teakwood panel, respond to the dappled light in a Renoir painting, and look in awe at the stained glass windows of a church. We ponder the somber dignity of the Vietnam Veterans Memorial in Washington, DC, or simply admire the natural beauty of a cloud formation in the sky. We have feelings and opinions about what we see, and make connections to traditions, customs, cultures, and each other. The power of art is discovering that each of us can learn from, appreciate, and create art. As Alberto says, "Even some people who don't know how are very good at art in their own way."

Art Is for Everyone

When my daughters Amanda and Pamela were growing up, making art was the work we did together. Our home was filled with paintings, collages, paper cutouts, clay tiles, and more. I remember Pamela planning art projects that would be the centerpiece of her birthday celebrations. I can still see children huddled intently around the dining room table reaching for fabric, paper, paints, and glue to create something wonderful—a doll, a mask, a painting. Our art-making tradition continues with my three-year-old granddaughter,

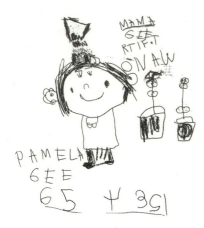

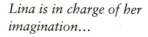

Lina is in charge of her imagination…

Lina. She sees a blank piece of paper and fearlessly uses bright colors, lines, and scribbles to symbolize her vision of dolphins swimming in the ocean. Ask her to tell you about her picture and Lina describes every detail and the significance of her marks on paper. Lina is in charge of her imagination, fitting ideas together, making connections, seeing relationships, and creating something new. She has found a way to express herself, and, like so many young children, is secure about her natural ability to make art.

In my role as an educator, I've tried to keep in mind the lessons learned from observing my children and granddaughter and a whole host of students as they make art in supportive, informal circumstances. I realize that working in trusting relationships with each other contributes to their independent thinking, spontaneity, comfort with experimentation, and self-confidence. All these qualities are necessary for a learner to feel safe in working with art. That realization, along with the belief that all people can be creative and do art, has guided my teaching decisions. As nine-year-old Javier tells us, "Art is for everybody who wants to do it." Indeed, children have a "can do" attitude when it comes to art, embracing the excitement that comes from making things.

Visual Arts in the Classroom: A Tool for Learning

We are becoming keenly aware that children can demonstrate classroom learning and understanding through art in ways that integrate intuition and cognition. Children draw upon forms of art to process knowledge and concepts. Through art, they're able to communicate ideas that show creativity of thought and the use of complex problem-solving strategies. As Pittsburgh-based visual arts specialist Valerie Dellas says, "Art is as valid a means of expressing our knowledge as the written or spoken word."

Bringing people together: an art-based service learning project. My friend and colleague, Alice Mendoza, now teaches at Captain Wilkes Elementary School on Bainbridge Island in Washington. Carrying pads and pencils, her third graders go on a botanical expedition, studying native Pacific Northwest plants and making careful observations. They render pencil drawings to record detailed observations, and they write notes about their observations. Back in the classroom, Mendoza invites children to view subject-related works of selected artists so students can become familiar with different expressive qualities and artistic styles. In a series of mini-lessons, she guides them to explore pen and ink as a drawing technique. As the children gain comfort with their newly acquired skills of observing and drawing, they create a series of pen and ink drawings of selected plants. Then, to create handmade black and white prints, they make an impression of their drawing onto foam core (actually redrawing it with a tool such as a pencil), cover the surface with paint, and place a clean piece of paper over the inked surface, smoothing the paper with a clean roller.

Students can demonstrate classroom learning and understanding through art in ways that integrate intuition and cognition.

Delighted with their artwork, Mendoza's students want to learn more. They research the names of their plants and write descriptions of the plants' culinary, medicinal, and ceremonial applications in the lives of Native Americans.

Field Notes: Teacher-To-Teacher

My classroom is a museum filled with the artifacts of learning. For my students, art has become a powerful tool for expressing their ideas, their interests, and their conclusions about the world around them. I display reproductions of fine art on the classroom walls to encourage children to create their own masterpieces. My students study the works and understand that the images in the paintings tell stories of people and cultures. They know that the way an artist chooses to represent the image has a dramatic impact on how they view and respond to the work.

Kerry Herrell
Alvarado Elementary School
San Francisco, California

The Washington children's research and artwork benefit two service projects.

They do their work with a sense of purpose and genuine enthusiasm, which are qualities Mendoza exudes in her teaching.

Mendoza asks her students to think about using their research and artwork to benefit two service projects—supporting education on Bainbridge Island's Nicaraguan sister island, Ometepe, and helping *Si a la Via* (Yes to Life), a grassroots project in Managua focused on providing care to homeless children. After a brainstorming session, the class decides to design, produce, and market a calendar featuring their writing, illustrations, and ink prints. These third graders had a grand scheme in mind—raising funds to build a one-room kindergarten in the small village of Urbaite, on Ometepe, and purchasing tools and materials for the *Si a la Via* center in Managua.

Mendoza's students wrote about the class project in the introduction to the calendar, "We have made a calendar of the plants of the Pacific Northwest and how the Native Americans used the plants." The students went on to provide background information on the two projects that would benefit from the sale of the calendar, and ended with "Remember that the children of Nicaragua are warm-hearted and friendly. They don't want our pity, they just need some help. When you buy our calendar, you are helping kids make a difference."

To date, five editions of calendars have been published. The cumulative profit of $20,000 has helped to fund three schools and a library on Ometepe and a basketball court and carpentry shop in Managua.

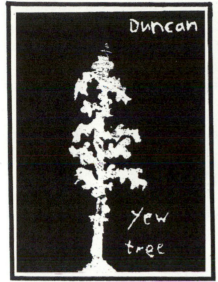 

Duncan

yew tree

yew branch

Western Yew/Pacific Yew was used for carving because it was heavy, tough and lasted a long time. Native Americans used the wood for bows, wedges, clubs, paddles and digging sticks. Today, there is a chemical in the bark called, 'taxol,' that is being used to treat cancer.

Students experience that their art can influence the way people feel.

Mendoza's students also benefit from their work on the calendar. She explains, "When kids sit down to do this calendar, they work really hard for a few weeks. Although the calendar theme is tied to classroom work, one of the strongest benefits for my students is they love helping children so far away. They learn that although our cultures are very different, we are all one people. On an artistic level, children experience that their art can influence the way people feel."

The quilting classroom. Many teachers I've worked with find that quiltmaking provides ways for children to explore an art form while gaining fine motor skills, connecting to their community, and enhancing their study of language arts, social studies and math. In Lexington, Kentucky, for example, children create and piece together individual patchwork squares to illustrate significant family stories.

In Compton, California, in Noel Wysinger's class at Carver Elementary School, a grandmother's oral history describes a way of life that seems almost fictional to an urban classroom of second graders. She captivates the children with stories of her childhood—hard field work on the farm, scant leisure hours spent sewing and making things. She passes around tufts of cotton, a well-preserved cotton plant, and remnants of her first quilt.

Indeed, as children handle the artifacts and analyze the quilt under the visiting grandmother's watchful eyes, they find a faded color scheme and the repetition of geometric shapes and patterns, marveling that history can be transformed into shapes and colors on cloth. They ask questions, and wonder aloud about what their lives would have been like "back then." With mounting enthusiasm, they calculate the number of squares to include in the class quilt and decide whether to make a paper quilt, a tissue paper quilt, or a fabric quilt. They're ready and eager to begin.

In classrooms like these where art is integrated with social studies, oral history, math, and geometry, intergenerational learning occurs naturally as grandparents and senior citizens become knowledgeable partners with students and teachers.

Field Notes: Teacher-To-Teacher

In a unit on immigration, we invited our students to interview their families about immigrant ancestors. The information gathered provided for some interesting conversation. For example, several students discovered they were named for one of their ancestors. Many students also learned about the clothing and hairstyles of their ancestors, as well as the work they did. In the interviews, students often heard funny stories, which in turn helped them learn that storytelling brings people alive—the stories contributed to the students' appreciation of their ancestors' humanness. After sharing the information they learned, each student drew a portrait of one ancestor to culminate this part of our unit. We featured the drawings on a bulletin board called "Portraits of Our Ancestors."

Joyce Caudill and Lisa Fulks
Kenwood Elementary School
Louisville, Kentucky

A geography connection. In Mary Tappan's third grade at Janson Elementary in Rosemead, California, children study the influence of various landforms and climates on culture and lifestyles as part of their Native American peoples studies. Tappan's students explore how food gathering and hunting is related to geography.

Because Janson is nestled in the San Gabriel Valley, Tappan and her students can observe the San Gabriel Mountains right from their schoolyard. Students quickly adopt "their mountains" and over the course of several days, gather outdoors with sketchpads to observe and draw. "Sketching the nearby landforms gives my students an opportunity to imagine how the native people lived and depended on their geographic surroundings for survival," says Tappan.

Once Tappan's students have completed their preliminary sketches, they analyze art prints Tappan has collected, and create watercolor landscapes from their sketches. She guides her students to see that artists have different ways of working and relating to a subject. This understanding helps children appreciate the uniqueness of their personal expressions. As ten-year-old Joyce

Students are eager and willing to pursue new learning because their interest and curiosity have been heightened through their involvement in art.

puts it, "I think art is a talent that everybody has in his or her own way. It makes me feel good because I made something in my own way that is beautiful."

Tappan tells me she is always delighted in the discoveries that individual children make about themselves through the visual arts. She also reflects on the interdisciplinary connections she can help children make. She sees that students are eager and willing to pursue new learning because their interest and curiosity have been heightened through their involvement in art. Tappan explains, "Using art as a tool for learning in my science and social studies curriculum has been very effective for my students' learning processes. They make connections easily between their artwork and social studies lessons, and they enjoy and take great pride in their work."

Understanding Natural, Creative, and Artistic Expression

Understanding youngsters' phases of development helps us anticipate students' needs as they develop their own interests and individual styles of expression. What knowledge do students bring to their art making? What skills might they need? Are they creating their work with an audience in mind? These are the questions to consider as children lift their paint brushes or get out their crayons or clay.

The terms *natural expression, creative expression*, and *artistic expression* refer to phases of artistic development. These phases overlap as each person finds individual ways of creating.

Natural expression. During the natural expression phase, students use their personal awareness of visual-spatial relationships as they draw, place colors on paper, or manipulate art materials. Students represent ideas and information based on their prior knowledge and exposure to visual expressions and symbols of art. What students have explored and experienced influences the forms of art they create.

Students gain increasing awareness that people may have different ways to judge the merit of a visual art form.

Creative expression. In this phase of their development, students focus on creative problem solving and participate in the process of making original works of art. They develop their natural abilities by learning about visual art elements such as line, shape, and color, and begin to arrange these elements according to principles of design such as balance, contrast, and dominance. They gain confidence in their interpretation of concepts and ideas as they apply skills, techniques, and methods to express themselves in a variety of art forms. They develop flexibility and sensitivity as they come to understand their own expressions and the artwork of others. Teachers help students gain insight into their work by reflecting on a theme, mood, and feelings the art communicates.

Artistic expression. In the artistic expression phase, students develop a sense of what an audience sees in their artwork. They understand the relationship between public taste and preferences and the influence of these on their own work. Their art-making becomes more individualistic and imaginative as they become aware of their personal choices and as they gain mastery over a range of skills and approaches. Students begin to appreciate the historical and cultural contexts for creating art and gain increasing awareness that people may have different ways to judge the merit of a visual art form. They understand that visual images can have lasting social importance, and that art is integrated into and influenced by life.

A Learning Continuum of Artistic Development

Artistic Phases	Characteristics	Drawing Examples
Natural Expression	• minimal formal instruction • students use prior knowledge and experiences	
Creative Expression	• facilitated learning about the elements of art and principles of design • students develop and apply art skills and techniques in original works • students begin to reflect on their own expressions and the artwork of others	
Artistic Expression	• students become aware of historical and cultural contexts and learn about making aesthetic judgments • students focus on mastery and personal style and on audience • students work to develop a high degree of artistic competence • students express and invent original approaches to making art • students understand the power of artistic expression	

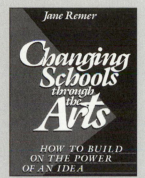
The Four Components of Art

Times have changed since educators considered the visual arts mainly as a skill in drawing, arts and crafts, or just something that was meant to be appreciated (Chapman 1978). Today we know a balanced approach that provides opportunities to create, look at, respond to, value, and appreciate the expressions of people across historical periods and cultural boundaries is likely to develop well-informed students who will understand ways the visual arts make us human. Since the *National Standards for Visual and Performing Arts Education* was published in 1994 and adopted in the *Goals 2000: Educate America Act*, forty-seven states have worked toward creating standards and implementing programs (American Music Conference 1997).

The *Visual and Performing Arts Framework for California Public Schools, K-12* (1996) defines a comprehensive arts program geared toward literacy in the arts. The document describes how visual arts as well as music, dance, and drama can each be studied from the perspective of four components: *artistic perception, creative expression, historical and cultural content*, and *aesthetic valuing*. Knowledge of the four components is useful for designing a balanced approach to learning in the visual arts and for developing critical thinking, inquiry, problem finding, and problem-solving skills in the arts as well as across the curriculum. I've found that students become very thoughtful about the way they think of visual expression when they have opportunities to integrate seeing, making, responding to, appreciating, and evaluating works.

Today we know a balanced approach that provides opportunities to create, look at, respond to, value, and appreciate the expressions of people across historical periods and cultural boundaries is likely to develop well-informed students who will understand ways the visual arts make us human.

Four Components of Art

In summary, the four components of art include the following.

1. Artistic Perception—seeing and responding to the visual makeup of artworks, including an understanding of the language of the visual arts.

2. Creative Expression—developing knowledge and skills to create, appreciate, and recognize the value of personal expressions and the creative work of others.

3. Historical and Cultural Context—gaining an understanding and appreciation of creative expressions across time and place, including the roles of artists, art objects, and images within both world culture and specific social contexts.

4. Aesthetic Valuing—learning to make qualitative judgments about artworks through thoughtful analysis of the works.

DIALOGUE

How will I encourage every child's development in the visual arts?

☐ provide time for mini-lessons and daily practice

☐ show images and artifacts from many periods of time and from diverse cultures

☐ create an art center with materials, tools, books, and other resources and provide time for independent research and practice

☐ encourage children with existing expertise to be "resident art tutors and coaches"

☐ invite community artists, art educators, and parents to provide expertise, demonstrate lessons, lead discussions, and plan meaningful enrichment activities

In what other ways can I support my students' learning?

_____

_____

_____

_____

SHOPTALK

Gardner, Howard. *The Arts and Human Development*. New York: Basic Books, 1994.

Gardner causes us to think of the arts as a tool for enhancing understanding—ideally, understanding is a central goal of education. This scholarly book—one of many that span Gardner's more than two decades of research and writing on the arts and human development—lays a foundation for us to think about how young learners create and appreciate art and how similar this process this is to that of practicing artists.

New Understandings About the Value of Art in Education

Art has been described as a universal language that provides all people with connections to other civilizations, and to past, present, and future cultures. Historically, there has been eloquent testimony about the importance of art; yet in many schools, art has remained an afterthought. In the last decade, educators have become increasingly aware of the multiple benefits that learning in and through the arts provides for all students. When, in 1983, researcher Howard Gardner published a theory of multiple intelligences—explaining that learners have at least seven intelligences (more recently he has identified an eighth intelligence) to explore, develop, and express themselves, we began to understand the importance of the arts as a tool for learning. Recently, David Perkins, a co-director with Howard Gardner of Project Zero—an educational research group at the Harvard University's Graduate School of Education—makes connections between the thoughtful consideration of art and the cultivation of thinking dispositions (Perkins 1994).

Teachers provide rich examples of what they learn about their students who are learning through the arts. They share insights about making the curriculum meaningful through regular inclusion of art and discuss the pride they feel as professionals who have found alternative ways for nurturing minds. For example, Karen Gallas of Lawrence School in Brookline, Massachusetts, believes her use of the arts—visual arts, drama, dance, music—in the curriculum moves beyond art as enhancement and enrichment. She follows her students' own expressive interests while using the artistic process—asking questions, generating answers, and coming up with new questions—as an integral part of expanding their knowledge in different ways. Sixth-grade teacher Lonny Ng at Anderson Elementary in Lawndale, California, believes her students

The artistic processess—asking questions, generating answers, and coming up with new questions—are an integral part of expanding students knowledge.

SHOPTALK

Perkins, David N. *The Intelligent Eye: Learning To Think by Looking at Art.* Santa Monica, California: The Getty Center for Education in the Arts, 1994.

David Perkins challenges all educators to think seriously about the connections between looking at and thinking about art to cultivate the habit of rigorous, reflective thinking in general. Rather than spending just a few moments looking at a work of art, Perkins suggests that we stop to take time to "see" art, to engage in the experience of enjoying, and to think deeply about the cultural, historical and social contexts expressed with works of art. He points out that we can learn to make a commitment to reflective thinking by giving works of art "looking time," and urges that we "look broadly and adventurously, look clearly and deeply, and look in an organized fashion." Thus looking at art can be a distinctive bridge to enhancing our ability to understand and think. Perkins provides all educators with new insights into theories about teaching and learning.

creatively and imaginatively solve problems through the arts. "They do things that I never thought of—my students push me creatively," says Ng. For example, she describes the process her students designed to illustrate their understanding of the insects they were studying in science. They created two-foot, three dimensional models of accurately drawn insects, with painted details of external body parts that could be lifted up to show the internal anatomy of the insects.

Using This Book

Visual Arts as a Way of Knowing is intended to help you become familiar and comfortable with some of the basics of integrating visual arts into your everyday classroom learning events. Throughout these pages, you'll find support that includes

- management strategies
- hints about tools, materials, and supplies
- approaches for facilitating drawing experiences
- lessons to help students learn the elements of art and principles of design
- ideas about assessing and evaluating progress
- examples of projects that integrate visual arts across the curriculum.

Some of the projects described in this book show ways to use visual arts as a means to develop deeper understanding across the curriculum, while others concentrate on art content, skills, and techniques. For example, you may find yourself helping students understand that culture is embedded in art by examining paintings depicting life in rural America, such as "Snap-the-Whip," by Winslow Homer.

"Snap the Whip" by Winslow Homer, 1872, Oil on canvas, 22 x 36 in.
The Butler Institute of American Art, Youngstown, Ohio.

To deepen students' grasp of science concepts such as change, students might make a series of observational drawings of time-related changes in plant propagation and growth.

Perhaps you will create mini-lessons to help students develop technical skill in their use of art elements. Over time, you will seek ways to deepen

SHOPTALK

Eisner, Elliot W. *Cognition and Curriculum: A Basis for Deciding What To Teach*. New York: Longman, 1982.

Whether you are an art educator, classroom teacher, or curriculum specialist, this resource is one to read and refer to as you plan your instructional program. Elliot Eisner fervently believes that the arts are basic in helping students with concept formation and meaning-making. He discusses the role of the senses and asks us to consider the contributions of visual, auditory, and kinesthetic "forms of representation." In other words, how are the visual arts, music, drama, and dance connected to human understanding? He creates provocative questions that we must ponder and explore as we try to integrate theory and practice in educational programs that help all children reach their full learning potential.

The arts are basic in helping students with concept formation and meaning-making.

their aesthetic awareness of their artwork as well as heighten their ability to evaluate the work of other artists. Art makes it possible to engage all students in learning across the curriculum. Art opens doors for all learners and invites them to use their imaginations for inquiry.

Just as important, you'll hear the voices of teachers describing their experiences. For those of you who are already integrating art into your curriculum, my hope is that you'll be interested in building on what you're already doing. And for those of you who are just getting started, my wish is that you will have no trepidation about picking up the tools of art to learn along with your students. For everyone, tap into the resources in your community including specialists, art organizations, and college art programs. The grand design for this book is to entice you to continue delving into visual arts and to make your journey and that of our students enriching and rewarding. Take advantage of new opportunities to explore, experiment, express, and evaluate your experiences with those of your colleagues and support each other in learning.

Chapter 2

Getting Started

Art is not just a project for school. It was made for different purposes. It is not just for kids. It can also be for adults.

Jacquely, age 9

Let's start integrating visual arts into your classroom. Creating a frame of mind and an environment that will allow you to work alongside your students is a good first step. Teachers have told me that sometimes it's helpful to think of themselves as beginners so they feel free to explore and experiment with art techniques, materials, and strategies. It takes practice to trust yourself and to look at your own work with "soft eyes," a term a colleague of mine, Adriane Bank, used to describe a gentle way of seeing any kind of new work you've produced. Doing this keeps us from being overly judgmental and allows us to reflect on the learning process rather than on the end product.

Think about art-making as a way to use a visual language. Instead of words, you'll be using a new visual arts vocabulary—elements of art—to communicate what you have in mind. We all have the potential to create with the visual arts. As respected artist and teacher Corita Kent wrote, "We can all talk, we can all write, and if the blocks are removed, we can all draw and paint and make things. Drawing, painting, and making things are natural human activities, but in many they remain in the seed state, as potentials or wishes."

To support your creative spirit, let's move from the "seed state" to experimenting and practice. Having loads of experience and expertise isn't required; you can begin with what you know, and build on that knowledge. Give yourself time to learn, and enjoy the process of solving problems using the rich vocabulary of the visual arts. If you pay attention to the possibilities inherent in creative problem solving, you'll learn more about your own creative process. In turn, your learning will help you guide your students toward finding original ways of expressing themselves in art.

As a teacher and artist-educator, I've been challenged regularly to move beyond my own safety net, taking risks and learning new ways to reach every student, all the while learning and having fun myself. In fact, just when I think I have become "expert" at something, a new theory, strategy, or way of thinking is uncovered, and I'm a beginner again. This is a great mind set for keeping artistically and intellectually stimulated, because I'm never sure what will happen!

The visual arts will add tools to your students toolboxes.

If you're going to guide yourself and others in doing art, I recommend remembering three things: 1) expect the unexpected; 2) find new challenges in every surprise; and 3) let the surprise suggest multiple solutions. Provide a creative environment that embraces the notion of work and play as one, and enjoy it yourself. In this atmosphere, your students will be more inclined to resolve problems in new ways rather than staying with what they already know, what you may want them to know, or what they consider to be the tried and traditional. As Mission Viejo, California, educator Faith Dennis says, "Being more open to children's ideas of how to solve visual problems has helped me grow as an art facilitator. Instead of imposing limits based only

Field Notes: Teacher-To-Teacher

I don't consider myself an artist, and I think we teachers tend to be threatened by the arts if we feel we're not artists or art experts. But I feel that if I hadn't taken the risk of bringing visual arts into my classroom, I would have done a disservice to my children. Incorporating visual arts in the classroom has helped to bring my class alive, adding tools to my students' learning toolboxes.

Julie Flanagan
William Anderson Elementary School
Lawndale, California

on my conception of a project, I ask students to suggest materials they might want or goals they might have."

Learning about something new or different isn't always easy. In the spirit of playful discovery, take the Artist's Pledge with your students and make a commitment to the process of uncovering the creative artist in yourselves.

Artist's Pledge

I promise to keep my eyes, mind, and ears open so that I will

- explore all ideas, materials, and methods

- be a fully engaged learner and risk-taker

- enjoy using my imagination

- follow my intuition and make connections between art and life.

Signature _____

Date _____

Setting Up a Personal Work Space

Take care to create your own personal work space at home or wherever you have a quiet place. Gathering the necessary supplies can be time well spent because you'll get ideas for managing visual arts in your classroom. At home, my art table is a hollow-core six-foot wooden door placed over two filing cabinets. I keep my most frequently used art tools and supplies clean and ready in containers on one side of the table. I use the file drawers to maintain a modest assortment of additional or special materials, tools, and resources. Although the room I use is tiny, it has a large window with good light, a wall for pinning up works in progress, and a wall of shelves that are overflowing with books, boxes, sources of things for making art, and portfolios of student art work. Everything I need is within my reach and ready to use. Granted, the size of the room doesn't allow for creating large-scale work, but I try out a lot of ideas, struggle with visual problems, write, and reflect in this designated "art space."

Here are some ideas for setting up an art space of your own:

- Clear a personal working space, perhaps a table near good light. Maintain a bulletin board or uncluttered wall space to pin up works-in-progress for reviewing as well as finished projects for appreciating.

- Gather a basic starter kit of art materials and place them in a cardboard box or large tray near your work table. Include crayons, a variety of pencils, two or three paint brushes, an assortment of felt-tip markers, watercolors, tempera paint, perhaps some oil pastels, and a bottle of black ink and pens with assorted points. Include some unconventional drawing tools—you can experiment with found objects such as straws, feathers, twigs, strips of cardboard, cotton swabs, small sponges, and toothpicks.
- Have accessible two or three stacks of drawing paper, construction paper, and recycled scrap paper in a range of sizes.
- Use a spiral notebook or blank sketchbook as a working journal for collecting ideas, jotting down sources, and writing down your reflections about your artwork.
- Begin collecting sources for making art—articles, magazines, pictures, images, found objects, writings, quotes, books about art, and so on.
- Keep a sponge and a few rags nearby for clean up.
- Find a large, sturdy cardboard box to use as a file cabinet or portfolio for your artwork. Since you will be keeping rough drafts of artwork—preliminary sketches, works-in-progress, samples of techniques and methods you've attempted, and final examples of work, you may want to make some dividers to separate your work into easy-to-find categories.

Organizing and Managing Art in Your Classroom

Infusing visual art into classroom learning requires organization, management skills, self-reflection, time, trust, and patience. *It means having access to art supplies any time, all the time.*

I remember that as a second-grade student, doing art meant that I could use crayons to color in the single mimeographed picture Miss Marcus handed out on Friday afternoon. I remember her ritual of walking up and down between the rows of desks, handing out one picture to each of us, then returning to the front of the room to unlock the cupboard where she kept the crayons. She passed the crayons out, admonishing us not to begin coloring until she gave the signal. We would all color in silence for the allotted time. I remember thinking that if this was art, I didn't want to do it.

Fortunately, I found refuge with my friend Marion in her uncle's print shop where we spent many wonderful afterschool hours imagining we were both artists and teachers. We had "tons" of paper, pencils, and printing inks to use in any way we liked. We made our own drawing tablets, set up a pretend classroom, and wrote and drew with carefree abandon and joy. I think just imagining what an effective classroom could be like and how it could be managed set the stage for my belief that the classroom and everything in it belongs to all learners and should never be locked up.

An environment that encourages art-making. Creating an environment that supports art-making helps demonstrate that you value art and see it as worthwhile. Fourth-grade teacher Julie Flanagan of Lawndale, California, places art supplies, books, magazines, art prints, and art-related resources on a table in full view of her students. They are invited to use the "art table" as regularly as the computer, dictionaries, reading books, math manipulatives, and other learning resources and tools in the room. In Mission Viejo, California, Faith Dennis often works alongside students on art projects. Dennis explains, "I want my students to see that I value and enjoy the act of creating art as much as they do. To model care and involvement in a project, sometimes I even ask them to wait a moment until I can finish a particular aspect of my own work before responding to their requests." Students in Alice Mendoza's class on Bainbridge Island, Washington, share responsibility for maintaining the materials on their art table because they value it as a prized resource in their classroom. They understand the laws of supply and demand, and take care to monitor themselves—conserving when necessary, and devising ways to be both practical and creative.

A cart of art supplies. To introduce her students to art materials and techniques, fourth-grade teacher Maureen Manning in Rosemead, California, sets out the materials on a rolling art cart placed near the front of the classroom. Manning spends about thirty minutes a day during the first few weeks of school demonstrating the use of oil pastels, watercolors, crayons, colored pencils, and other media she wants her students to try. While she provides feedback and encouragement, her students practice skills and techniques in a number of mini-projects to gain comfort and confidence. As the year progresses Manning gives her students plenty of time to explore and experiment with new art materials, media, and art forms, providing ways for them to express themselves through murals, picture books, illustrations, and sculpted forms as well as through technology. The student artists take on added responsibility for maintaining the art cart and act as mentors to each other.

Obtaining Art Supplies and Other Resources

A common fear among teachers is that they won't know what to buy or how to shop for art materials. I recommend planning ahead and combining budgets with a few colleagues in order to purchase materials in bulk and increase your buying power. In the meantime, however, you needn't be concerned if your materials are the most basic: a stick dipped in ink can be used for drawing, and recycled cardboard and corrugated paper make terrific surfaces for painting. It's helpful to know that outstanding images of art throughout history and from diverse cultures are available in art prints, slides, videotapes and CD-ROMs. Contact the education departments of your local library and museums for information about their resources.

Designing an art area is an integral part of making art an accessible force in your classroom.

Involving Your Community

Even without a budget set aside for art materials, the basic materials you can collect are just the beginning. I'm a great believer in the art of the pen when writing letters asking for art materials we need for projects. You and your students can write to let the local business community, parents, friends, and service groups know that their donations of time, talents, goods, and dollars can

---

Field Notes: Teacher-To-Teacher

If you want your students to feel like artists, they have to become artists—even if it is just for that moment. Building a creative classroom environment invites your students to feel safe in expressing themselves artistically. Designing an art area is an integral part of making art an accessible force in your classroom. I have an art table in my classroom: on it there are scissors, paints and paint brushes, palettes, markers, pencils, a vise grip, and reusable paper scraps. Nearby is a cubby stocked with additional paints and tools such as hammers, screwdrivers, and saws.

> Kerry Herrell
> Alvarado Elementary School
> San Francisco, California

enrich learning opportunities. Make sure you invite all involved parties to attend events where students display their art projects. Acknowledge the support you receive from others and include this support, as appropriate, in your announcements of events, bulletin board displays, and discussions with students.

Your own community is often the best place to start your search for resources. With a little bit of research, you might be pleasantly surprised at what you find. In the San Francisco Bay Area, for example, there is a non-profit organization called Scroungers' Center for Reusable Art Parts (SCRAP) open to the community. For a nominal fee, teachers can fill a paper shopping bag full of materials. SCRAP solicits and accepts donations from stores, small factories, and business offices. Materials contributed have included thread and fabric, paper of all sorts, wire, wood, yarn, film cans, sheet plastic, foam core board, dishes, clothing, buttons, costume jewelry, and even old appliances.

Enlist the help of others. Sande Leigh, principal at Harvey Milk Civil Rights Academy in San Francisco, actively seeks out innovative ways to help her faculty obtain materials to supplement their basic school supplies. She writes mini-proposals to purchase art supplies, contacts merchants in her neighborhood for extra help, and seeks out community artists and family volunteers to help support the faculty in bringing art into the classroom. Leigh is a very persuasive art advocate who once recruited me into a lunch hour of collecting empty shoe boxes from a neighborhood shoe store that the children transformed into stunning memory boxes of family life artifacts.

Field Notes: Teacher-To-Teacher

During my first few years of teaching, I kept the crayons out in a large ice cream bucket so students would have easy access to them. The paints and other art supplies were put away in a cabinet. I was the only one who could remove them. I came to realize that students would not use what they could not see or touch. Space was limited, so I searched for ways to make supplies available. A deep window sill provided space in one classroom. In another room, I used empty cubbyholes with brightly colored baskets to organize our art supplies—actually, our "arts" supplies, because other baskets held musical instruments and costumes for drama. Once the students began to see the materials, their ideas never stopped. They were always eager to try something else.

Sherry Fortenberry
Mendenhall Elementary School
Mendenhall, Mississippi

If you have a chance to attend a state or national art conference, such as the annual National Art Education Association Conference, you'll have opportunities to network, attend lively sessions, find excellent literature and resources, and receive sample art materials and handouts that provide good information about sources of resources.

Buy materials in bulk. Search for the best deals in your area's arts and crafts stores and remember to buy in bulk. Individual pans of watercolor can be purchased by the dozen and distributed as needed. This conserves the amount of paint used and keeps the watercolor box from getting too messy. Felt-tip markers can also be purchased in bulk. They can be sorted by color and stored in plastic bags, plastic boxes, or tins.

Saving and organizing materials. Just as important as obtaining materials is keeping what you have in good shape and ready to use. Encourage conservation: cut scraps into different sizes and model ways to use them appropriately. To promote order, ask students to sort papers by color, size, and type. Then save all paper scraps and unused materials in shoeboxes or similar containers.

A large cardboard box or sturdy crate with dividers can serve as a table-top filing cabinet for pictures, articles, and reference materials. Enlist the help of students, parents, and colleagues in adding to your cache of art reproductions, magazines, postcards, calendars, museum catalogs, articles, and pamphlets for making art and extending interests. Ask students to help with cataloging, filing materials, and decorating their storage boxes.

Getting To Know and Care for Art Tools and Supplies

The power or effectiveness of childrens' art projects often depends on the art tools and supplies they use.

Paper and other painting surfaces. You and your students needn't confine yourselves to the standard 9"x 12" sheet of paper. Use different sizes, shapes, thicknesses, and colors of paper or other materials for drawing and painting. Move beyond using only flat surfaces. Explore the possibilities of working on textured surfaces such as light sandpaper, corrugated cardboard, discarded boxes, and scraps of fabric. Look into transforming two-dimensional pictures and designs into three-dimensional forms. Think about drawing and painting on geometric forms such as cylinders and squares. Found objects and recycled materials can be used to create delightful art pieces and images.

With your help, students can stretch their imaginations and consider everything they see as a source for making art.

With your help, students can stretch their imaginations and consider everything they see as a source for making art. You can model this for them by looking at everything around you with an eye for its potential as an artist's medium.

Field Notes: Teacher-To-Teacher

After researching the African rainforest, students worked in cooperative groups to construct our classroom rainforest. The students designed plants and animals of the rainforest using crayons, clay, and recycled materials of all sorts. All kinds of old paper, leftover paint that students mixed, and scrap supplies the parents sent in—cereal boxes and cans, empty spools, leftover yarn, newspapers, feathers, and old pipe cleaners—were among the wide range of media we used. Our odds and ends helped students create a layering effect that really captured the look of a rainforest. Trees are hung from the ceiling making a canopy for the plants and animals that lived within the layered branches of the tree.

Joyce Caudill and Lisa Fulks
Kenwood Elementary School
Louisville, Kentucky

DIALOGUE

How will I provide a safe environment for students to experiment?

_____

_____

How can a variety of materials and techniques help students
explore and take risks?

_____

_____

Brushes, paint, and other tools of the trade. You need the right brush for the job, so try to keep an assortment on hand. Remember that the number of a brush corresponds with its size—the smaller the number, the smaller the size. Brushes come in different shapes as well. Generally speaking, round and flat brushes made of sable or acrylic hairs are good for watercolor, tempera, acrylic paint, and ink. Round and flat bristle brushes are also available— they're good for using with tempera and acrylic paint. When cleaning brushes, the most important step is to remove all the paint with soap and water. Finish the process with a thorough rinsing and drying. Store brushes flat on a tray or upright in a coffee can or jar.

Everyday objects can be used for holding paint and storing materials. You can use a muffin tin or plastic egg carton for holding tempera paint while you work. Cover the unused paint tightly with plastic wrap or aluminum foil for storage. Small yogurt cartons make excellent water containers, and a plastic or paper plate with a waxed surface works well as a mixing palette. Keep paper towels nearby to blot your brushes. Also keep two large containers handy, one with clean water and one for disposing dirty water; clean your brushes after every use.

Felt-tip markers come in a variety of sizes. They are pointed, chiseled, fine, or broad-tipped. Water-based markers are safe for classroom use. Should the markers dry out, dip the tips in water to rejuvenate them.

Oil pastels produce both vibrant and soft-color effects. Use a thick pad of newspaper under your work to cushion the surface for a smooth, even application of color. Watercolor can be used with oil pastel to produce a technique called wax resist. The trick to keeping the watercolors bright and sparkling is to use water sparingly as the color is brushed over oil pastel.

Pens and pencils. Dip pens and pens with changeable nibs provide interesting effects when used with drawing ink. Pen work requires practice and guidance but its expressive possibilities make the effort worthwhile. Drawing inks are available in many colors, although black is the most commonly used. Water-soluble ink can be used with dip pens, drawing sticks, and soft brushes.

Graphite pencils come in degrees of hardness and softness. The 9H is the hardest and makes the lightest line. The 7B pencil is the softest and makes fuzzy, blurred, darker lines.

The most commonly recommended pencils for drawing in elementary school are the 2B, 4B, and 6B. Their varying degrees of softness enable students to gain control over the quality of line they use when drawing.

Clay play. Students learn a great deal handling clay, by just seeing something creative evolve in their hands. The forgiving nature of clay makes it the perfect medium for starting over: if we don't like what emerges, we simply squeeze the clay into a ball, slap the bubbles out of it, reshape it, and begin again.

Keep a large covered bin of clay in the classroom for everyday exploration as well as for special ceramic projects. Clay comes in a variety of forms—choose according to the purposes you have in mind. Usually, moist blocks of clay work well for most projects. Water-based clay comes in reddish-brown or grayish-white tones that can be fired in a kiln, with or without a glaze. If you don't plan on firing the finished pieces, slightly damp clay objects can be coated with white glue to produce a glossy finish and protect their shapes. Caution students to handle unfired pieces carefully, however, because without firing the clay objects will be fragile.

More About Clay

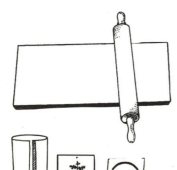

Clay can be pinched, pulled, molded, and rolled into a slab. With pinching, pulling, and slab methods, students can create all types of hand-built forms—pots, candleholders, bowls, cups, animals, tiles, vases, figures—just about anything you can imagine. One of the easiest ways for learning about the properties of clay is to allow students time for "mushing" around with the clay before attempting to work with it. Gradually, they'll shape things with their hands and feel the art object coming together before their eyes. Following is some basic information about clay.

- Clay comes in dry powder or in 25-pound moist water-based form.

- Real clay-making tools come in various sizes and are highly useful implements. They're durable and students appreciate working with the real thing. These tools can be supplemented with plastic forks, knives, nails of various sizes, rolling pins, and popsicle sticks.

- Pieces of burlap or canvas of about 24-inch squares placed on top of cafeteria trays create a good surface for working with clay—the clay won't stick.

- Use a rolling pin to roll out slabs of clay that can be cut and formed into tiles, cylinders, or other shapes.

- Found objects or other collectibles can create texture and interest when pressed into the clay.

- A length of wire or a nylon fishing line slices easily through a block of clay. Fasten the wire to two round sticks to use as handles.

- An airtight plastic pail with a lid works well for storing unused clay.

SHOPTALK

Baumgardner, Jeannette Mahan. *60 Art Projects for Children: Painting, Clay, Puppets, Prints, Masks, and More.* New York: Clarkson Potter, 1993.

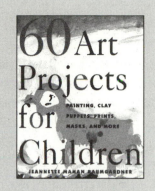

Baumgardner provides guidance to teachers and parents who want to nurture children's self-esteem and natural creative instincts. As artist and parent, Baumgardner helps you build on your knowledge of handcrafts and explains the importance of carrying on the tradition with young children. She writes about the value of the physical experience and the skills that come with making conscious modifications while creating objects. The projects offered in this book will give you some great ideas to use in your classroom.

Who Is Responsible for Taking Care of Supplies?

Artist, teacher, and friend Karen Wright of Santa Fe, New Mexico, helps preschoolers and kindergartners understand that art materials can be magic in their hands. She also teaches students to respect and care for the tools of creativity. Students become experts in art and learn to take good care of oil pastels—which can take a serious beating if they aren't kept clean. Taking great pride in their efforts, students wipe each oil pastel with a tissue, organize them by color families, and replace the pastels neatly in their boxes. They practice sorting skills by stacking papers according to size, texture, and color; and they're able to categorize drawing tools by type. Wright taught me how to create a supply table that is a marvel of colorful organization and a help to students as they practice being independent and responsible. With colored tape to designate the appropriate places for items such as crayons, markers, scissors, and paper, you can create sections marked with shapes and hand-printed signs so that students are able to recognize and read the names of all the items they use.

When students share responsibility for designing and maintaining the art work space, they not only enjoy it, but also learn some important lessons about courtesy and respect. They'll take particular pride in being your "extra set of eyes" as they search for opportunities to include art, collect resources, install the classroom gallery, and keep things tidy. As Adam, one of my more spirited fifth graders used to say, "It's got to be neat and look aesthetically pleasing because we all work better that way."

Students who share responsibility for maintaining the art work space learn important lessons about courtesy and respect.

Students like to "work smarter." I've found they enjoy taking responsibility for their actions. Housekeeping charts help them keep track of duties they have agreed to do, and provide a way for group evaluation. Not surprisingly, this awareness promotes some important learnings about the art of management, the theory of supply and demand, conservation, surveying, and data collection. Before making their "Art Housekeeping Chart," students can generate a list of guidelines for taking care of materials, discuss how they want the room to look and sound, and work out standards for what is acceptable. I'm pleased to see many students concentrate on their work. With a little practice, they like clearing their desks to create personal work spaces and consistently honor the rules they set for themselves. Their self-monitoring actually helps them cut down on waste, and they can gain at least ten additional minutes of work time. In turn, their art-making activities take on a higher level of intensity and purpose.

As the master designer of your classroom environment, you decide what will work for you and your students. But you'll benefit from asking students to help design work spaces and brainstorm the kinds of art projects, artists, and cultures they would like to explore. Give them opportunities to teach you about their interests. Once you and students start looking at the multiple uses of art in your classroom, you'll be surprised at how different your learning environment will become.

Art HouseKeeping Chart			
Responsibilities	Distribution	Clean-up	Evaluation
paper	Mark	Sally	✓+
paints	Juan Mary	Juan	⊕ terrific
brushes	Jessica	Bill	✓— could be cleaner
palettes	Laurel		
scissors	Miguel	Mark	✓+
clay			
books	—		
other supplies	Essie	Du	✓+
environment		whole class	very good ✓+

DIALOGUE

In what ways do I provide opportunities and motivation for students to extend their interests in learning about art?

_____

_____

In what ways do I encourage students to pursue their interests?

_____

_____

In what ways do I invite students to help in making art possible?

_____

_____

In what ways do I ensure the lessons learned in art transfer to lifelong learning skills?

_____

_____

Becoming the Facilitator

Doing art is not a mystery, but getting started can sometimes be a little intimidating if you feel you lack the necessary time, knowledge, or skills. When classroom teacher Jan Cohn (who worked with me at Seeds University Elementary School in Los Angeles) began teaching art, we partnered up so that I could actively support her as she guided students. We often taught side-by-side, and Cohn asked many questions. Sometimes she worked on a project alongside our students while I facilitated the lesson, and other times she took the lead while I observed and provided feedback to coach her on what she wanted to learn. We found this was a mutually beneficial way to learn from each other: she gained a great deal of confidence and expertise, and learned valuable strategies for sharing information and uncovering talent. Our collaboration enhanced my ability to reflect on my own teaching and make adjustments to be more effective. Cohn's interest and enthusiasm for integrating visual arts has continued and grown as she has delved more deeply into her own artistic development.

Visual arts and drama specialist Stephanie Mathis at Brentwood Elementary in Jacksonville, Florida, helps teachers build art connections from the suggested learning events in the Galef Institute's *Different Ways of Knowing* curriculum modules. She helps teachers make visual arts become more tangible in the classroom. "There's a more conscious effort by teachers to come to me for ideas and strategies for using art in the classroom. Teachers tell me what students are studying, and I work with them and their students on related art and drama activities."

Linda Migliore, who teaches first grade at Emma W. Shuey School in Rosemead, California, said that after she began integrating visual arts regularly in the classroom, her natural talent and creativity reemerged, and she decided to take a weekend painting class.

Haven't you found that when something gives you personal satisfaction and pleasure, you want to share your enthusiasm with your students? Think about the various experiences you've had with art—books you've read, museums and galleries you've visited, and leisure-time art activities you enjoy. Take a few moments to write down what you already know about art, how you feel about what you know, and what more you'd like to know. Putting your thoughts to paper can put you closer in touch with the steps you might take to include art in your classroom.

Understanding Process and Product

Perhaps this is a good place to mention that as you and your students make art, you'll have to trust a process that encourages intuitive thinking. Because visual art relies on seeing relationships and making connections, decisions about what to do next depend on working with imagery from moment to moment. Trust your instincts as you get better at cultivating the way you look at parts in relationship to the whole image or object you're creating, and remember that the creative process unfolds slowly. Be careful not to prejudge or limit your own process or those of your students. Much of the creative problem solving in visual art happens as you integrate the formal art elements such as line, shape, color, and texture with your sense of imagery. You and your students will draft and redraft, each of you using your own sense of space. You'll pause to consider the visual effect and the impact of your work. Is it pleasing? Is it powerful and strong? Encourage students to ask themselves thoughtful questions about their work by modeling the process yourself. What do I want to show? Do I get my feelings across? What idea or message am I communicating? Like a poet who artfully arranges words, phrases, and sentences, the artist chooses and arranges visual elements to communicate.

DIALOGUE

What do I know about the visual arts?

_____

_____

How do I feel about what I know?

_____

_____

What do I want to learn more about?

_____

_____

Who can support me in my efforts to learn?

_____

_____

Kidwatching and reserving judgment. I once learned a stunning lesson from ten-year-old Amy, who had joined my fifth-grade class halfway through the school year. I had given the class an assignment of painting a still life of velvety-red geraniums, placed in a watering can and positioned on a high stool. Children found their places around the still life, and they confidently shared hints and openly discussed how they would begin using the tempera paints to create their paintings. Amy, however, walked around the still life several times, touched the geraniums and then went back to her seat. Brush in hand, she dipped it into every color of tempera available—red, yellow, black, and white—and began scrubbing her paper with paint. Startled, I watched and waited in silence. The other children remained engrossed in their work. Amy proceeded to put her fingers in the paint until both hands were fully covered, and then she rubbed her hands over her paper using her fingers as brushes to paint stripes and swirls across the page. I asked Amy to tell me what she was seeing and to talk about her picture. She said she had never painted before and didn't like what she had put on the paper, but believed that she had to feel the paint. She didn't think she had "messed up," but would like to try doing some more art until it "felt right." I listened in wonder as Amy, in a perfectly reasonable fashion, assessed what she needed.

Even though it sometimes takes lots of restraint to reserve judgment, kidwatching is a powerful and valuable tool.

Since you'll be using art as a tool for learning and as a means of self-expression across the curriculum, you'll want to remember that not all of the work needs to result in a final product. Some students may use art to help them form ideas. Others may return to complete their work or to develop their ideas by writing stories or poems.

The "Art" of Being Prepared

Knowing that children's personal experiences with art will vary, we want to provide a supportive environment that encourages them to truly explore, beginning with what they already know and gradually developing their confidence and skills. Now when I plan for any visual arts learning, I make sure to ask myself these questions:

- How will I provide ample time for free exploration of materials?
- How will I assess each student's emerging creative needs?
- What can I learn from observing without judging?
- What kind of coaching statements can I make to guide all students?
- In what ways do strategies in facilitating visual arts transfer to effective teaching and learning practices across the curriculum?

Reflection: Part of the Process

Thoughtful, creative energy goes into the process of making art. Your written reflections can help clarify and define your journey as a developing artist and facilitator of art experiences. Begin by writing down your goals and expectations, and reflect upon your personal interests. As you work on various lessons and mini-projects, write down what you are learning that makes art accessible. Think about what you are enjoying or finding to be difficult; note as well what you are discovering about yourself as a learner. What questions do you have? What will you learn next?

Just as kidwatching and reflection help us learn about what our students know and are able to do, self-reflection offers students a view into their own learning. At the end of each work session, I ask students to evaluate

- what they like about the assignment they have just completed
- what they have learned
- what they want to improve
- what they want to learn next.

Now that we're in an "art frame of mind," we're ready to explore approaches to drawing.

Chapter 3

Everybody Wants To Draw

Imagination is a picture in your head that shows you what you are thinking about and it's a wonderful thing to do.

Marvin, age 9

We draw to express what we see and what we imagine. We draw to tell stories, to make diagrams, and to sketch projects we want to undertake or objects we plan to make. We draw to entertain ourselves and others, to express ourselves when words simply aren't enough. There are many reasons for drawing, and yet many people hesitate. Why? My guess is that the hesitation comes from insufficient opportunities to develop the skills of seeing and drawing.

You'll want to be sensitive to the opportunities your students may or may not have had to express themselves through drawing. To increase their awareness of size, shape, and textures, ask students to hold and really feel objects. For example, before asking students to draw a tree, have them go out and look at one, feeling the texture of the trunk, smelling the bark, and perhaps putting their arms around it to get a sense of its girth. Ask students to notice the shapes of branches and to look for variation within the leaves.

In a similar way, with your help, children can become aware of composition and the placement of figures and objects within a picture surface. When I see students placing the green stripe of grass at the bottom of the page and the blue stripe of sky at the top, complete with a yellow sun in the corner, I know it's time to take them on observational walks to see the variation of colors in the sky and what fills the space between sky and ground. I like to show the work of different landscape artists so students can develop their awareness of the wide variations of interpretation of natural settings as well as ways to use space. Then I ask them to solve the problems they find in their own pictures.

Looking To See and To Draw

Seeing is very different from just looking.

Look at something you see and you can draw it. Remember, as artist Corita Kent said, "Everything we see becomes a source for making art." Seeing is very different from just looking. As you guide your students to see, they'll find that images are everywhere—some pretty, some not; some mundane, some exciting. How we respond to, understand, and interpret these images is, of course, determined by our points of reference and our ways of seeing. It isn't surprising when we understand something, we "get the picture" and say, "I see."

Field Notes: Teacher-To-Teacher

As a compulsive art postcard purchaser, I can stop by a museum shop and buy an affordable collection of paintings and drawings in a matter of minutes. I found long ago that postcards of museum-quality artwork serve as good models for helping students practice the art of seeing and drawing. Students are naturally inclined to look for and see details and expressive qualities they may want in their own drawings when they use these models. In addition, the small reproductions are a convenient size that makes viewing the work manageable. After some initial guidance, drawing from postcards can be completed as independent work, with students taking their time to replicate the models. I have sometimes asked students to transform the small-scale drawings into large-scale works. Notably, I've found that students make stylistic distinctions between the two sizes.

–KG

Field Notes: Teacher-To-Teacher

When we are practicing drawing in the classroom, I tell students to spend a few minutes clearing their tables of books and materials from other studies, and selecting paper and pencils and other art supplies to create an individual "art studio." I play soft music in the background to help with the "changing of gears," and students tell me that the process of preparing their mental state and their physical space has a calming effect that prepares them for focusing on new work.

–KG

You'll find that drawing what you see will follow naturally if you s-l-o-w down the process. Using the basic element of line, we can all draw what we see. There isn't a right way or a wrong way to use line, nor is there a right way or a wrong way to draw. As artists, we all have creative choices in how we choose to use line. (The element of line is explored more fully in Chapter 4.)

The tools you use will have an effect on the appearance of your drawing. I like to begin drawing with a medium-soft lead pencil because it is portable and flexible. I make sure that I'm open-minded about what will emerge and I don't worry about erasures. I don't think about the name of the object or the label of the subject I'm drawing. Instead, I concentrate on seeing and trust intuitively that the seeing will guide my hand to record the image on paper.

At times, you'll help students acquire specific skills and techniques in drawing, such as contour and observational drawing. When students have a foundation from which to begin making artistic choices, you are empowering them to have control over the work they produce. I've found that giving students guidance in drawing and encouraging them to draw in sketch journals as a free-choice activity enhances their willingness to practice and to set goals for personal improvement.

Warming-up. A good warm-up exercise for students is to take a sheet of paper and spend a few minutes exploring drawing with pencil. Ask students to be conscious that they are making different kinds of lines and notice that the lines can intersect, loop and magically become shapes. Have students pay attention to how they push and pull the pencil around the paper. They

can turn the paper at different angles, but ask students not to raise the point of the pencil. Play with scribbles and swirls, and curved, straight, jagged, thick, and thin lines. See if students can use the pencil lightly, or on its side. Ask them to notice what happens when lines overlap.

On another occasion, have students experiment with a variety of drawing tools. They'll be able to see the different visual effects that pencils, markers, and ballpoint pens allow them to achieve. For example, ask students to look for thick or flowing lines in comparison to thin and straight lines. After they've covered the paper with lines, ask students to pick out areas where they felt they had the most control.

To begin to develop a line vocabulary, invite students to name or describe the types of lines they've made such as curvy, scratchy, and jagged, and record the information on a chart. You can have them include visual examples, and you'll have the beginning of a common vocabulary for everyone in the class. Post the chart as a reference point and source of inspiration for future exploration and development.

Drawing upside-down. Betty Edwards suggests that upside-down drawing helps children and adults relax and focus on lines, shapes, and spaces rather than on the subject matter of the drawing (1979). Upside-down drawing is particularly helpful if you feel you can't draw, since the focus is on seeing, developing concentration, and working slowly and deliberately. Edwards calls this "drawing at a snail's pace." I've asked students who felt they had no artistic talent to try upside-down drawing. Students doing this exercise concentrate on seeing relationships between the lines and spaces of the image, paying much less attention to their ideas of what the image should look like.

After practicing this kind of drawing, both you and your students will gain confidence and successfully move on to contour and other types of drawing.

To get students started, I generally suggest trying a black-line upside-down drawing of something from nature. Drawing simple plant forms with well defined shapes and structures is less intimidating than drawing a person. You might like using postcards or reproductions of fine art drawings for this exercise. Whatever you choose, this drawing activity should be straightforward, with few tonal or textural effects, so that students can concentrate on seeing and putting down lines.

Place the picture upside down, and put a blank sheet of paper on top of it, leaving about two inches of the image showing. Have students draw on the blank page the lines they see, moving horizontally from left to right across the page. Gradually they can move the paper down to reveal more of the image and continue to draw, matching up lines and taking note of the relationships between lines and spaces. Remind students they aren't tracing the picture; they are "seeing" the lines and spaces in the picture and recording them as accurately as possible. You'll find students concentrate very hard on what they see rather than worrying about what the picture will look like. It's important to be nonjudgemental. When their drawings are complete, allow time to talk about what surprised them.

Drawing upside down helps children relax and focus on lines, shapes, and spaces rather than on the subject matter of the drawing.

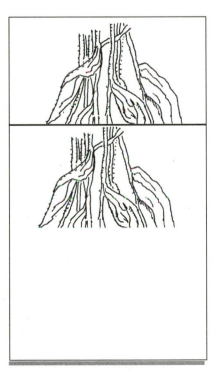

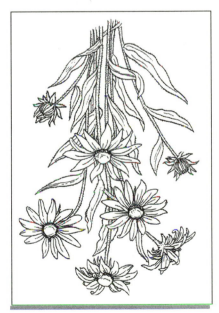

In blind contour drawing, you look closely at the object you are drawing—not at your paper or the drawing you are making.

Practicing Contour Drawing

All contour drawings are made with lines that show the edges, or outline, of objects. In blind contour drawing, you look closely at the object you are drawing—not at your paper or the drawing you are making. The direct simplicity of contour drawing is exciting, forcing you to suspend judgment as you draw. Blind contour drawing enables us to draw by seeing, trusting that our eyes will guide our hands and drawing tools.

When you begin contour drawing, keep three points in mind:

- slow down and let what you see guide your work
- match up lines and pay attention to the spaces between the lines
- trust your intuition to make choices about what you see.

Choose an everyday object with some degree of complexity and character such as a familiar shoe. Ask students to close their eyes and slowly feel the contour of the object, running their fingers along all of its edges. After a minute or so, tell them to open their eyes and see the object, paying close attention to every detail, every edge. Next, they must decide on a point of view. Will they look at their shoes, for example, at an angle, straight on, from the side, or from the top or bottom? Ask students to decide on a starting point and, using a soft pencil or felt-tip marker, to draw the object slowly, letting their eyes guide their pencils and hands. Remind students to keep their eyes on the object, drawing very slowly to capture all the edges in contour line.

I like six- and seven-year-old students to start off with fine-point, felt-tip markers when they begin contour drawing. The markers allow the children to create fluid lines and see their drawing emerge on paper more clearly than with pencil. I usually provide black or brown markers and encourage a lot of exploration so that students are comfortable with the medium. Older students draw well with either markers or soft pencils. I recommend teaching students to manipulate the amount of pressure and weight they place on their marker or pencil; the pressure affects the quality of what they produce in their drawings.

If you or your students draw an unwanted line, treat it as an opportunity rather than a mistake. Draw over or through the line to incorporate it in the image. If you are using pencils and must erase, do it sparingly. Coach your students to look at their work as a way of finding and solving problems, and encourage them to have an open mind about the process.

Field Notes: Teacher-To-Teacher

I've found that sometimes students are not pleased with a piece of art they have produced. One way I've been able to help students see their work positively is to crop the picture with pieces of construction paper. We move the pieces around until we find a part that the student likes. With the student's permission, I trim the picture so that only the selected area remains, and then the student mounts that section on another piece of paper and adds to it or enjoys it as it is. A piece of art that was headed for the trash becomes a prized possession!

Sherry Fortenberry
Mendenhall Elementary School
Mendenhall, Mississippi

Contour Drawing with Young Children

I asked Lynn Shelley and Susan Caruso, teachers of a primary multiage classroom in Lawndale, California, to help me explore contour drawing that is slightly different from blind contour drawing in that you may glance periodically at the object you are drawing. Shelly and Caruso agreed because they were eager to identify strategies to increase levels of engagement and nurture artistic talent in all of their students. They gave themselves the task of kidwatching while I guided the drawing lesson.

I distributed large sheets of paper and markers to students, explained what we were going to do, and asked them to take part in a few warm-up exercises to flex their drawing fingers. I invited them to talk about their favorite shoes and tell me what they thought about them. Then I asked them to take off one of their shoes. Students removed their shoes with lots of giggles, and I asked them to seek out every bump, crack, and crevice of their shoes with their fingers. Students described what they saw and felt—rubber, ties, velcro, bumpy, red—as I recorded their words on a chart to create a working vocabulary for further development in arts activities.

The students placed their shoes on the table in front of their work space and began drawing full-sized representations. Some students became fascinated with shoelaces or patterns on the undersides of their shoes, drawing every detail very slowly. Others drew very quickly, but with gentle urging attended to recording additional details. Most concentrated on the drawing activity for close to forty minutes. During that time, you could have heard the proverbial pin drop. We asked students to walk around and see all the emerging drawings—there were lots of smiles, "thumbs-up" signals, and exclamations of pleasure. At the end of the drawing time, students told us they had learned that everybody could draw and they were proud of how hard and long they had worked. We asked students to imagine moving out to recess

---

DIALOGUE

What drawing skills do I observe in my students?

_____

_____

How can I help students build on their strengths?

_____

_____

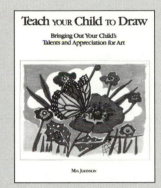
Children can learn to think, see, and feel like artists when they draw.

in ways their shoes suggested. With laughter and high spirits, the children explored different ways of moving. A student wearing cowboy boots tried galloping, another child walked with feather-like steps because she was wearing pastel-colored canvas shoes, and several children demonstrated basketball jumps and moves because they were wearing high-top gym shoes.

Being reflective and responsive teachers, Shelley and Caruso gained new insights into teaching and learning from this art experience they wanted to explore further, such as

- different intelligences and learning styles
- management and coaching strategies that empower all students
- high expectations for all learners
- kidwatching techniques to assess learning.

Practicing Observational Drawing

Once you and your students are comfortable with blind contour or contour drawings, you'll want to try observational drawing. In observational drawing, an artist's focus is not only on the visual characteristics of objects but also on their relationship to other objects in a setting.

When you try observational drawing,

- be keenly observant
- choose a point of view from which to observe what you draw
- slow down to observe subtleties
- look at the object you're drawing and at the drawing itself, and continue to add details.

Think of observational drawing as a process of seeing, observing, and recording visual data. Concentration and "looking to see" are skills worth developing across the curriculum.

Drawing Indoors

Begin observational drawing inside the classroom by setting up a still-life arrangement with a small number of objects. As you begin assembling objects to arrange in a setting, think about how they relate to one another, offering interesting contrasts of size and shape. You may want to gather some objects to create a visual theme or simply find a selection of items on your desktop that appear to be a "natural" still life. Other possibilities include a collection of children's toys or even an assortment of objects that have no apparent relationship to one another.

Keep these things in mind when setting up your still life:

- decide on placement—a table, chair, or the floor
- select a small number of objects
- vary size, shape, height, and width of objects
- place objects on a sheet of paper or a cloth to isolate the still life from other things in the room
- place objects so they overlap to create a sense of space.

Concentration and "looking to see" are skills worth developing across the curriculum.

Ask students to think about what point of view they'll take when they begin to draw. For example, will they make their observational drawing by positioning themselves so that they look at the still life straight on? Will their point of view be from the side, at an angle, looking down on the still life, or up at it? Artists make decisions all the time about viewpoint; it can inspire different ways of seeing the still life as they draw. You'll often find that artists draw the same objects repeatedly, from a variety of viewpoints, because they are able to see a range of artistic possibilities and learn from each one.

Eating and drawing apples. Visual arts educator Pamela Considine of Crossroads School in Santa Monica, California, likes to use apples or other fruits and vegetables as the subject of observational drawing. Considine often uses just one fruit—rather than a number of objects—so that she can coach and provide guided practice as students develop art techniques and skills with different media. For this next exercise, she likes students to use colored pencils.

For homework, she invites each student to bring in an apple with color variations, such as a Macintosh, Gala, or Braeburn. She makes sure to have some extras on hand, and draws with her students throughout the exercise. Considine gives each student five 6 x 6-inch squares of paper and asks them to tape them

Field Notes: Teacher-To-Teacher

Recently my class received some goldfish. I asked the children to observe the fish carefully for five minutes, noting as many details as possible. After writing down their observations in their journals, the children drew the fish. They captured the subtleties they had observed. Drawing helped the children see that observation and concentration are skills that are necessary in representational art.

Kerry Herrell
Alvarado Elementary School
San Francisco, California

Careful observation is as integral to visual arts as it is to observing phenomena in science.

together lengthwise. She also provides some scrap paper. The apples will be drawn in five stages of change, one picture per square of paper, beginning with a drawing of the whole apple and continuing at various stages of its being eaten. In the final square, all that remains is the core.

Because these drawings take a while to do and demonstrate change over a period of time, I like to think of making connections to science. Careful observation is as integral to visual arts as it is to observing phenomena in science.

In science, for example, you might ask students what changes they think will occur because of the apple's exposure to air in the environment? How will covering the apple with plastic wrap, aluminum foil, or brown paper between bites and drawings change the shape and appearance of the apple? Students can be encouraged to make hypotheses and predictions.

The students put a sheet of paper on the table and place the apple on it. They feel the apple's shape carefully before deciding on a point of view. They look at it closely and slowly, observing all its details. In the first square, they make a full-sized observational pencil drawing of the apple. Once they've drawn the apple, they consider it carefully again, pick it up, and take one or two bites. Then they replace the apple on the sheet of paper, observe the shape of their bites and how they changed the apple's overall appearance, and draw it in the second square. The students continue to eat their apples, "sculpting" them as they like.

Drawing vegetables, plants, shells, and crinkled paper. As you and your students practice observational drawing, invite them to bring in objects they find interesting to look at and to arrange their own still lifes. Vegetables, plants, shells, crinkled paper, and recycled objects are great to use as subjects. Items such as these help students see that ordinary things have extraordinary potential as sources of artwork. Drawing everyday objects also helps train the eye to see unexpected relationships and details, and is a good way to practice different techniques for creating shadows and the illusion of depth. Have students draw exactly what they see, noticing tones and variations. Remember, objects can be drawn singly or in an arrangement. Once you have provided the whole class with practice in observational drawing, you can establish a learning center. Refresh it occasionally with new objects, paper, and pencils for individual students to use to practice and enjoy their new skill of seeing and drawing.

Looking at lighting. Light causes shadows and highlights, helping to define the shapes and forms of objects. Side-lighting (from the left or the right; either a little below or above the arrangement) provides a soft glow, while back-lighting creates deep shadows in front. It's worth remembering that a light source aimed directly at the still life tends to flatten objects out. If natural lighting—light from the outside—is not available, create lighting effects with a desk lamp or large flashlight placed about three feet from a still-life arrangement. Try bouncing the light from a lamp off a wall or piece of foam core onto the subject.

Drawing negative space. When does nothing help you define something? Drawing negative space helps strengthen your ability to see. Let's see how this works. Set up several items for a still life on top of a sheet of paper. Now place a sheet of paper  behind the objects, creating a backdrop. As you look at the objects, take special care to consider the spaces and shapes around and between them. See these spaces as negative shapes with as much importance as the objects, or positive shapes. Draw only the negative spaces using a marker or pencil. You can fill in the negative spaces to help you focus on seeing them as shapes that more clearly define the outline of the objects in your still life.

Making self-portraits or portraits of family members. Portraits are a wonderful way to explore drawing, and they can be done with children as young as seven. Encourage students to draw their faces or those of a family member, full size on large sheets of drawing paper. When making portraits, have students start by making slow, observational drawings, and pay attention to all the details. If they are making self-portraits, have them use large hand mirrors to look at their faces straight on. Have them bring in photos for portraits of family members. Encourage them to concentrate on the features of the face, studying, observing, and drawing full-size every detail of what they see.

Draw eyes first, then eyebrows. Direct students to notice the direction and quality of the lines and shapes of the eyebrows, eyelids, lashes, nose, nostrils, lips—even the spaces between their features. Draw the lines that indicate the shape of the face and the ears, and the hair that grows out from the scalp. Above all, encourage students to draw slowly and dispassionately, without concern about whether their work is a likeness of the real person. Gradually, the likeness will emerge. Many portraits are quite elegant as line drawings.

Drawing Outdoors

You can integrate observational drawing with field trips by having students take along their sketch journals and pause to make careful drawings. Combine note-taking with drawing to help students remember their perceptions and significant facts.

Outdoor drawing requires a little preparation. Students can use a large sketch pad or portable drawing board (a heavy sheet of 20 x 24-inch cardboard

with a string wrapped tightly across the top and several sheets of paper slipped underneath the string will work). The strategies that apply to drawing objects indoors apply to outdoor drawing as well. Take note, though, that the lighting effects, due to change in the atmosphere and time of day, vary the appearance of objects arranged outdoors. Use this as an opportunity for making connections to your science studies.

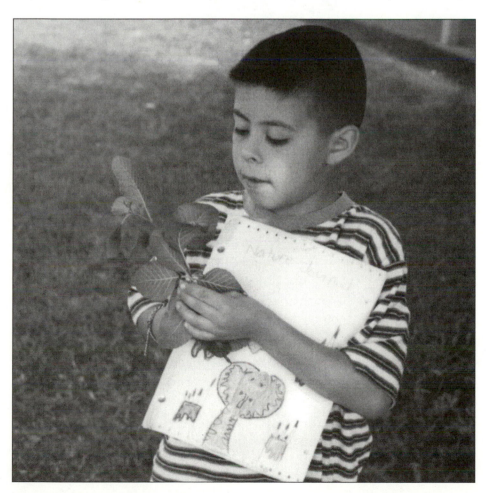

Find something students want to draw and a comfortable place to work. Then begin by observing the objects in the environment and their relationships to things around them—good subjects include trees, buildings, architectural details, and close-ups of interesting objects found on an observational walk or the school grounds. Landscapes, as well as city street scenes, are also excellent subjects for practicing observational drawing outdoors. I encourage students to use a viewfinder to help them isolate and edit what they want to include in their compositions. A simple way to make a viewfinder is to fold a piece of paper in half and cut a one-inch square in the center. This is very similar to a viewfinder in a camera. The size and shape of the paper you use will also influence what you include in your picture.

Quick drawing, sketching, and gesture drawing are surprisingly similar to pre-writing strategies.

Quick Drawing, Sketching, and Gesture Drawing

To draw when we need and want to draw, we should have multiple strategies, portable tools, and materials on hand to put down the images that suddenly inspire us. Here are three easy strategies to help you and your students capture initial ideas, ones that you can explore in depth over time after the image is captured. Unlike contour or observational drawings that are slow and deliberate, quick drawing, sketching, and gesture drawing are like visual shorthand, serving as techniques for getting down the basic structure of a scene or object you see and want to remember. You may be surprised at how similar these strategies are to pre-writing strategies. Quick drawing, sketching, and gesture drawing are appropriate if students need or would like to learn alternative methods for getting ideas down quickly.

Field Notes: Teacher-To-Teacher

The natural world gives us great stimulus for all kinds of learning. Whether in the classroom or outdoors, visual arts provide a way for students to look at the world with fresh eyes, develop observation skills, demonstrate what they know, and reflect on powerful experiences. Although most drawings my fourth and fifth graders do are accompanied by writing, the drawings also enable children with limited writing skills to express complex understandings. This is important in any class, but particularly valuable in our "inclusion" class of children with reading levels ranging from grades one through eight.

Amika Kemmler Ernst
Manning Elementary School
Boston, Massachusetts

Quick drawing. I like making quick drawings because they help me in putting down a lot of visual information or something that seems important to me at the moment, without worrying too much about drawing every detail. Quick drawing is quick annotation done by using loose lines and a few scribbles. It can be done with pencils, pens, and markers. I jot down what I see and use words and phrases to help me remember the rest of the image. You might think of quick drawing as a way of taking mental notes in a visual-symbolic form. Let's say students and I are doing a river study, and we take a field trip. We want to keep a record of the plants we see along the bank so

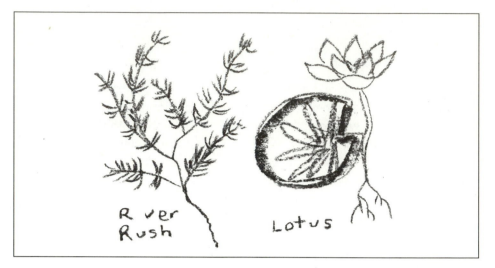

we can identify them later. This is the time for quick drawing. However, don't be surprised if your students prefer to take their time while drawing because they become engrossed in the process.

Sketching. We make sketches to capture general impressions or ideas of what we see or have in mind. You can use sketching to lay out the way objects relate to each other in a picture and work out the way you'll compose a picture. If you're designing an outfit or costume, you'll sketch the general structure but not necessarily all the details. You can use light pencil or chalk for sketching. Think of sketching as a way to prepare for a future drawing or painting. You can rework the sketch into a final drawing. Our river study includes ways people are using the river. Here's a sketch of what we found.

Gesture drawing. As the term implies, you use large, loose, fluid lines in gesture drawing to capture movement, letting your whole arm move freely in dance-like motions. Think of gesture drawing as action drawing and look for the relaxed and free quality of line that you produce with this kind of drawing. For making large-scale gesture drawings, use large sheets of craft paper, a large soft paint brush and watercolor, or a wide sponge brush dipped in tempera. Here is my gesture drawing of the river flowing.

Drawing in Perspective

How do you get an illusion of three-dimensional space in a two-dimensional drawing? How do you make objects and forms in a drawing look realistic? The answer is through the use of linear perspective, which was perfected during the Renaissance by European artists. The Italian, Giotto, was the first artist who consistently created the illusion of depth in his paintings. Soon after, other painters became influenced by his work. Views of interior rooms, buildings, and street scenes, and the visual changes that occur to make forms in the scenes appear realistic started to emerge in the painters' works.

In Western art, there are two types of perspective. *Linear perspective* closely fits the way people see objects and forms in space. This connection is probably why we are in awe of drawings that appear "real." Basically, parallel lines that we 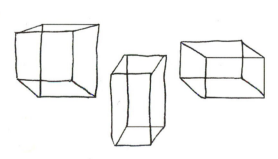 see in the foreground seem to converge at a vanishing point on the horizon. Objects appear smaller as their distance from the eye increases. *Atmospheric perspective* means that objects in the distance appear fuzzy or out of focus. Not surprisingly, understanding perspective in general helps establish the scale of objects and why they appear smaller as they move farther away. Knowledge of perspective comes in handy when you begin to look for ways to create the illusion of depth in your drawings.

Nowadays, many artists take a much more relaxed attitude about the traditional rules of linear perspective: different ways have been invented to manipulate the structure of space and the illusion of depth through the use of color, texture, and other art elements. Consequently, we have choices about how to guide our students to an understanding of the rules of perspective so they can apply them in their own drawings. I like providing a balance between a technical method—using rulers, marking lines, and drawing three-dimensional boxes, and a more informal method—helping students see the value of overlapping to create depth and dimension (Wilson 1987). Simply put, one object is placed either in front or in back of another, partially obscuring it. You can use artworks that depict crowds as a model, or have students draw a series of repeated shapes to help them understand the idea.

Here are some guidelines to think about when working with perspective:

- Objects of the same size look smaller in the distance.
- Objects nearby are detailed, and become less detailed as they recede in space.
- Overlapping creates the illusion of depth.
- The horizon always appears at the artist's eye level.
- A vanishing point is located on the horizon.
- Color fades as it moves into the distance.

Students are eager to learn how to represent depth and dimension. Providing them with practice in a few basic drawing techniques, as illustrated in the following chart will help them get started.

Basic Techniques for Representing Depth and Dimension		
Technique	**Visual Illusion**	**Example**
Overlapping Overlap objects in a sequence on the same plane	Objects seem to be sequential and grouped on a common implied line	
Overlap objects behind one another so objects get progressively smaller	Objects seem to move back in a space	
Foreground, Middleground, Background Objects in front are larger, and more detailed than those in the background	Picture or image seems to have depth	
Light and Dark Light colors	Light moves objects toward a viewer	
Dark colors	Dark causes objects to recede	
Contrasts of dark and light, bright colors, and tones	Creates depth, or dramatic effects	
Hatching and Crosshatching Sets of parallel lines	Creates volume, density, or shadows	
Shading Using gradations of black or color give the effect of dimension and volume	Creates highlights and shadows in objects	

S H O P T A L K

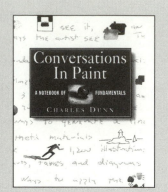

Dunn, Charles. *Conversations in Paint: A Notebook of Fundamentals*. New York: Workman Publishing Company, 1995.

A terrific resource I've found to guide my basic understanding and use of perspective is a book by Charles Dunn called *Conversations in Paint: A Notebook of Fundamentals*. Don't be fooled by the title; Dunn provides a simple and practical way to help you with one-, two-, and three-point perspective. Excellent step-by-step illustrations show how uncomplicated the theory actually is in practice. There are other principles of design and tips on painting that you will enjoy as well.

You and students are just beginning to see the possibilities that drawing offers. I recommend that you and students do a little drawing every day. Why not carry a sketch pad to capture images that move you in some way? Look carefully at drawings in museums, art galleries, and books. Study drawings, think about them, and talk about the qualities you see in different drawings to get ideas for trying out new things. Remember, everyone can learn to draw, and that art is a lifelong learning activity you and students can continually pursue.

Soon you'll be applying knowledge of the elements of art and principles of design you'll learn about in the next chapters to your drawings as well as to other forms of art.

Chapter 4
Art Elements

An artist has skill. Artists are not scared to try things. Artists have imagination and interest in their work. They do not rush through their work.

Leonardo, age 8

Art is about communication. As writers and speakers, we use verbal language to communicate. We make choices about the content, choose the theme, decide on the vocabulary and form of communication we'll use to express ourselves. We hunt for just the right words, look at nuances and relationships, and make decisions about the structure and form of our communication. Will I write a poem, essay, short story, or a speech? How will I organize my words and phrases to have the most impact? Artists make the same choices about how they work, but use a visual vocabulary to express themselves. This visual vocabulary, also known as *art elements,* includes line, texture, shape, space, and color. Try to imagine the art elements as parts of speech—the nouns, verbs, adjectives, and adverbs we use selectively to organize ways in which we communicate.

In addition, we use the *principles of design* to help organize our visual composition. The design principles include balance, dominance, contrast, repetition, rhythm, variation, and unity. They provide us guidelines for using the art elements. We'll discuss and demonstrate the principles of design in Chapter 5.

In this chapter you'll find ideas for experimenting with the art elements. Try out the approaches and share your creative insights and intuitive leaps with your students as you guide their explorations. You and your students will use different tools, materials, and techniques to create, describe, analyze, and assess your work as you go along.

I like to organize art lessons into a four-part process which I call the Four E's—Exploring, Experimenting, Expressing, and Evaluating. In this way, I make sure that students

- explore concepts or skills to see what they already know
- experiment with new skills, materials, and techniques to discover and understand what new methods will offer them
- express their thoughts and ideas in creative and aesthetically pleasing art forms
- evaluate the learning process and products of their work to reflect on how they've met artistic challenges.

The art elements are like parts of speech—the nouns, verbs, adjectives, and adverbs we use selectively to organize ways in which we communicate.

Field Notes: Teacher-To-Teacher

When I worked as a site coordinator for an artist-in-residence program in Arkansas, I had many opportunities to see young students making creative discoveries. At the end of a one-day art workshop, I was packing up my art supplies and getting ready to go home when a boy of about nine years, ran up to me holding a still-wet clay and wood sculpture in his hands. He grabbed my shirt and said enthusiastically, "I'll need some more red paint tomorrow and maybe some yellow." I turned to him and explained that the workshop was only for that one day, and he began to cry. He looked at me and said, "But I can't learn all I need to know in one day." I wished I had a videotape to capture that moment so I could share with educators, artists, and funders how art is so much more than content and skills, that children experience things that are deeply moving to them, and that doing art also brings self reliance, compassion, and a sense of community.

Karen DeJarnette
Director of Research
The Galef Institute

The Language of Lines

Lines define shape, delineate where things are, lead your eye, and take you from one place to another. What are lines? If you remember signing on the "dotted line," then you'll know that lines start with dots that can travel in any direction, varying in size, thickness, darkness, and lightness. You can make a line with any implement—your finger or a brush dipped in paint, a twig, pencil, pen, or piece of chalk. You can draw lines in space without making a mark on paper, and viewers will follow the direction of the invisible lines with their eyes. You can say what you want with curved, jagged, broken, straight, and repeated lines; and you've already discovered the importance of lines in drawing in Chapter 3. You can be explicit with outlines or see implied lines when edges of shapes appear to touch, such as when you look at a row of books lined up on a shelf. Lines also help to give directionality and a feeling of depth in two-dimensional works.

Exploring Lines

When I first introduce line to students, I ask them to notice the lines that their bodies can make. Have everyone raise one of their arms in a half circle to create a curved line. What kinds of lines can students make with their legs? their torsos? This kind of exercise will help focus students and allow you to see what kinds of lines they are familiar with. I also read or ask

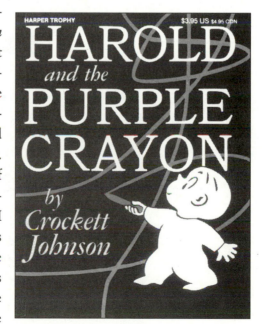

students to read the classic storybook *Harold and the Purple Crayon* by Crockett Johnson. They see that Harold's lines take him on many adventures—slaying a dragon in the forest, sailing on the ocean, ballooning over mountain tops, and building a city, to name a few. Harold is an old artist friend of mine and soon becomes one of students' favorite characters. Then I ask students to take note of the lines in our everyday environment. We brainstorm as a class or in groups to come up with a beginning line list. Students make lists of where they see lines and write down words that describe the qualities of the lines they see or imagine at school, in their neighborhoods, and at home. Here's a partial list of descriptive words to get you started on creating a line chart: arched, scribbled, jagged, thick, thin, spiral, broken, blurred, feathery, vertical, parallel, and textured. What line descriptors can you and students add to the list?

Going on a line hunt: looking to see. Alice Mendoza of Captain Wilkes School on Bainbridge Island, Washington, believes in helping learners develop their artists' eyes. In coming to know the element of line, her students go on a "line hunt" and make line books with their discoveries. The students make simple sketchbooks and take periodic walks with Mendoza around the school grounds to hunt for lines in the environment. They look everywhere for lines, and draw them in their sketchbooks with pencils and markers.

In the process, students develop a keen awareness of the different qualities of line. Suddenly, cracks in the sidewalk, textured lines made by bricks in the wall, vertical lines in doorways, horizontal lines on a window pane, line patterns emerging from wood grain, and the cross-hatched lines of a chain-link fence come into sharp focus as art elements. Students sometimes write or dictate descriptions of their observations, and the element of line takes on a concrete, physical meaning for them. What begins as a lesson on seeing and identifying the visual qualities of line becomes the context for building concepts in language as well. The line hunt paves the way for learning more about lines and about artists who use line as a dominant feature of their work.

What begins as a lesson on seeing and identifying the visual qualities of line becomes the context for building concepts in language as well.

If the only language or symbols you could use to communicate were lines, you would still have a lot to say.

Experimenting with Lines

What if lines could talk? They can. If the only language or symbols you could use to communicate were lines, you would still have a lot to say. Let's try talking in lines through drawing. Ask students to recreate the following passage in the "language of lines" using what they already know, referring to the line chart they've made, or inventing some new lines.

> From a dreary, sunless sky, snow fell gently on my front yard, covering the shrubs like mounds of cotton candy. Two stately trees stood on either side of the front gate with their bare, spindly branches reaching upward. A string of lights twinkled off in the distance and I heard the sharp, resounding bark of my neighbor's dog across the way.

Give students several unlined 3 x 5 inch index cards to retell the passage in line. Students often find index cards less intimidating than a full sheet of paper, and they can try out many variations on different cards. Have students experiment with different drawing and painting tools they're familiar with to see what visual effects please them. When students have made several of these "studies in line," ask them to arrange them on a large sheet of construction paper to see the results. Groups of four students can then place their work side by side on the floor or the wall to explore arrangement, or composition. This may lead to some students wanting to redo or add to one or more of their drawings to make their composition what they envision.

Line Mini-Projects

When students are comfortable using lines to express themselves, they can increase their creative options by experimenting with a variety of tools, techniques, and materials. I like planning a series of mini-projects so that students develop skill with techniques and materials. Ask students to keep a portfolio of their work so they can assess their development, reflect on their progress, and see the visual effects they are learning to achieve. (We'll discuss portfolios and other reflection/assessment techniques in Chapter 6.)

Let students use an array of mediums to learn and to discover their personal preferences. On many different days, have them try felt-tip markers, then watercolors, and mixed media techniques with pen and ink combined with crayons and other media. Each medium will provide an interesting change of pace and give students a repertoire of expressive tools.

Plan ahead to manage classroom art lessons and projects so that all students feel successful and *you* feel comfortable. In the beginning, set aside about forty-five minutes to demonstrate a new approach and enough time for practice so that you can observe, encourage, and provide feedback to each child. Then leave materials out so that students can continue to practice on their own.

DIALOGUE

What do I need to practice before I demonstrate a new technique or skill?

_____

_____

What coaching can a parent, volunteer, another teacher, or visual artist provide me and my students?

_____

_____

What agreements have I made with my students to promote independent learning?

_____

_____

What do I expect my students to know and be able to do once they have completed their mini-project?

_____

_____

Expressing with Lines

Have students try the projects listed below on different sizes, colors, and shapes of paper. I like starting off with a 6 x 6 inch square, gradually increasing the size along the way, so that students become aware that changes in size and format influence their artistic decisions. The squares translate nicely into cubes that students can construct once they cover the surfaces with line designs. Encourage students to try different combinations of lines and create "never-before-imagined" line patterns. They can experiment with the element of line by creating designs using

- black lines on white paper
- black lines on colored paper
- painting white lines on black paper
- cutting lines out of strips of paper and gluing them down, like a collage
- using thick, puffy lines interspersed with fine lines
- working on paper batik (see the description that follows).

Exploration of materials. To make "puffy" paint, mix equal parts of salt, water, and flour. Divide the mixture into separate dishes and add drops of food coloring or spoons of powdered tempera to get desired colors. Pour the mixture into squeeze bottles, one color per bottle, Students use the paint by gently squeezing it onto paper.

For paper batik, cut brown paper bags into workable sizes. Crumple the paper up, then smooth it out slightly with a warm iron. Use crayons—dark colors such as brown and black work particularly well—to draw line designs on the crumpled paper. Place the completed drawing crayon-side down on several stacks of blank newspaper, and iron gently. The melted-crayon design will be a little blurred and have the appearance of batik. If you gently crumple the brown paper, it will eventually become soft like fabric and can then be used for creating simple costumes and accessories. This activity works well when parents or other volunteers work with students. Volunteers can do the ironing and then make their own paper batik, right along with students.

Studying an art element in isolation enables students to gain an appreciation for its versatility in all artwork.

Our goal is to provide many different opportunities for students to expand their own "line vocabulary," which will in turn enhance their drawings, paintings, and designs. Studying line in isolation enables students to gain an appreciation for its versatility as an art element in all artwork.

Getting Smarter about Lines

One of the best things about art is that as you practice, you continually get smarter about different mediums and techniques. Students gain a great sense of freedom and enjoy the challenges in finding new answers and ways of expressing themselves. To help students get smarter in the use of line, give them lots of opportunities to practice. For example, create challenges for your students by

- placing color limitations on projects so students focus on the impact of line as an expressive element
- introducing textured surfaces for painting and drawing, such as sandpaper, crinkled aluminum foil, corrugated cardboard, and surfaces already bearing line patterns, such as the classified section of a newspaper
- transforming two-dimensional expressions into three-dimensional forms using toothpicks, straws, wire, wooden dowels, pipe cleaners, cardboard, and stiff paper strips
- painting cityscapes, landscapes, or other subjects using only vertical, horizontal, and diagonal lines
- creating the illusion of texture by inventing new ways to use tools and techniques (see the chart on page 73 for examples).

Evaluating Your Line Work

Don't forget the importance of class critiques during projects and following their completion. Use opportunities to help students reflect on the qualities they appreciate in their work and to talk about what they've learned in the process. Try to include preliminary studies along with final products. Students can critique work in pairs or in groups of four; individual students can write about a piece; or the whole class can look at and discuss work on display. During class critiques, ask students to

- use descriptive vocabulary to talk about the expressive qualities they see in a piece of art. You might prompt students with questions like: Look at the lines and the colors in this piece; what do you think the artist is feeling? What pleases you the most about the lines in this piece of art?

- discuss the creative problem-solving strategies the student artist may have used to create a piece of art

- discuss what skills and techniques students may want to develop next to create another version in their studies on a particular subject

- discuss what additional art prints and resources may help them deepen and expand their understanding of line and other art elements.

SHOPTALK

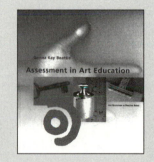

Beattie, Donna Kay. *Assessment in Art Education.* Art Education in Practice Series. Worcester, Massachusetts: Davis Publications, 1997.

Marilyn G. Stewart, the editor of this series, writes that it "provides the art teacher, museum educator, student, scholar, and layperson involved in art education with an overview of significant topics in art education theory and practice." Beattie's book provides the most recent developments in research and theory brought together in a clear presentation of what a practicing teacher needs to know about assessment in art. The author shows that assessment need not be limited to tests: indeed, performance assessment strategies—including portfolios, art journals, and a multitude of integrated performance options—are detailed and evaluated. This comprehensive book provides the information you need to make informed decisions about art assessment in your classroom.

"Cataract 3, 1967" by Bridget Riley. Used by permission of the artist and the British Council Collection.

Creating Visual Textures

The art element of texture can be a dominant feature in a painting, drawing, and other art forms. We generally think of texture as a quality we can feel as well as see, both tactile and visual. You might introduce texture to students by having them rub their fingers against sandpaper or an emery board and ask them to describe how it feels. Then explain that they'll be learning ways to recreate a surface that appears rough, sandy, or grainy using the elements of line and shape.

Students can share what they already know about textures. They can gather objects from school, home, and the outdoors to make a class collection of textured objects. Some of my students have made tree rubbings and brought in sea shells and cotton balls, as examples of texture. How about asking students to look in the crisper of their refrigerators for textured food? They can gather broccoli, parsley, and celery, to name a few. Ask them to look at a slice of bread for texture. They can also use their sketchbooks to draw and describe textures found in nature.

Capturing textures in art forms. Ask children to think about how textures such as tree bark, flowers, stems, and pebbles might be replicated in pencil, crayon, pen and ink, or paints.

To capture an object's texture on paper, ask students to place a clean sheet of white paper over each of the objects they've collected and make a series of pencil or crayon rubbings. To help students develop their "texture" vocabulary, you and your students may also wish to experiment with a variety of materials and techniques like those in the chart below to create textured effects. Our goal is to sharpen students' awareness of texture and its usefulness as an art element for adding interest to their artwork.

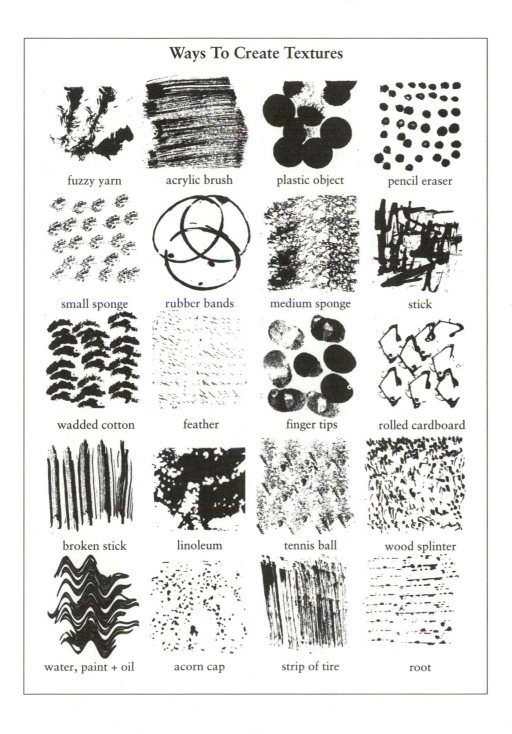

Ways To Create Textures

fuzzy yarn	acrylic brush	plastic object	pencil eraser
small sponge	rubber bands	medium sponge	stick
wadded cotton	feather	finger tips	rolled cardboard
broken stick	linoleum	tennis ball	wood splinter
water, paint + oil	acorn cap	strip of tire	root

Field Notes: Teacher-To-Teacher

A clever child once told me to look at the zillions of tiny lines and patterns I had on my hands. I did, and she was right: there were lots of lines in the palms of my weather-beaten hands as well as on the backs of them. I began drawing the intricate patterns they made, seeing my wrinkles as decorative lines and texture—a rewarding way of seeing wrinkles! From that moment on, any time students would tell me they had run out of inspiration, I advised them to check out their hands and use their imaginations.

–KG

Experimenting with Textures

A great way to learn about and create visual texture is to experiment with ideas that pop into your head. After you've been at this awhile, you and students will have developed a repertoire of techniques to integrate textures into drawings, paintings, and designs. Students enjoy creating texture notebooks, going on texture hunts, feeling and tasting textures, and inventing ways to show texture in their work. Use some of the following ideas to get students started.

- To make instant texture, crumple up paper and smooth it out with your hands. Voilá—you have a textured surface on which to draw or paint. To add more texture to the surface, you might take pen and ink or soft pencil and draw different lines in each of the spaces created by the crumpled lines. Try to get a visual sense of depth and density.

- Blow up a balloon and let the air out of it. Feel the texture in the deflated balloon, then use a soft, colored pencil to re-create the texture you observed.

- Tape together two or three drawing tools—such as a pencil, crayon, and ballpoint pen—and make stippled (dotted or speckled) lines with your new drawing tool. Decide on some motif, perhaps "v"s, and create a line texture.

- Take the side of a soft pencil (2 or 4B) and cover a small surface with pencil strokes, spreading the tone evenly. You can create a smooth, satiny surface by rubbing a cotton ball or soft tissue over the pencil markings.

- Add a little thinned white glue and fine sand to tempera or acrylic paint to create a grainy texture.

- Create a mystery texture box by placing different textural objects inside a sturdy box. Cut a large hole at one end of the box, large enough for a hand to reach inside to feel each object. Ask students to draw or paint what they feel.

Rob Bell, a former teaching colleague of mine from Seeds University Elementary School in Los Angeles, California, noticed that his students always represented grass with one broad, horizontal stroke of green across the bottom of the paper. Here he saw a good opportunity to integrate science with art. First Bell asked students to speculate on different varieties of grass, how and under what conditions they grow, and to make hypotheses about whether grass grows sideways as their drawings indicated. Students carried their study of grass outdoors. Armed with drawing boards, paper, and pencils, Bell and his students sat on a grassy area outside of their classroom to observe blades of grass using what he called "our x-ray eyes." He asked them to feel the blades of grass with their fingers, one blade at a time, and to use all of their senses to speculate why texture, lines, directionality, variation, and color were important in their artistic representation of grass. Rising to the occasion, students drew and drew and drew—except for Rudy who sat feeling the grass slowly, one blade at a time, drawing nothing. When Bell asked what he was doing, Rudy replied earnestly, "Touching texture first, looking second, drawing last."

From Lines to Shapes and Spaces

Remember, lines begin as a series of dots moving off in any direction you wish. When the lines close or converge, you create shapes. You can recognize shapes as people, plants, animals, and objects. There are *organic* shapes, those found in nature, and *inorganic* shapes, those manufactured such as tables, chairs, pots, and telephones. You're already familiar with myriad *geometric* shapes— circles, squares, pentagons, cylinders, pyramids, and cones. When you focus on shapes, you'll notice that their outlines vary. Shapes can appear crisp and hard; soft, blurred and curvilinear; or robust, heavy, and voluminous. Some shapes remind us of particular feelings and emotions. For example, the heart shape is one that's become a popular icon for romance or love. Shapes sometimes look solid. They may be open forms that you can look into or through. Shapes can be made with lines or blobs of paint. When a shape is arranged in a space it becomes a *positive* shape and the space around it is a *negative* shape or negative space (see page 53 in Chapter 3).

Shape Explorations

Students can start out exploring shapes by painting blobs with tempera or watercolor. Next they can draw raw shapes or outlines and fill these in with pencils, markers, and crayons. They can use scissors to cut out shapes free-hand, without first drawing them, and later sculpt a similiar shape out of clay. Remind students to use the human form as a source for creating shapes such as the hand, lips, ears, and eyes. As you and students gather more information about shapes, it may be very helpful to make a shape chart, as you did with lines and textures, to keep track of your discoveries. You'll want to pay attention to the infinite variety of edges your shapes can have, and to look at where one shape begins and another one ends. Shapes can be tiny or huge; they can exist inside other shapes; they can stand alone, overlap, or touch. Shapes are flat or three-dimensional, and it's great fun to experiment with creating large, free-standing shapes. You'll find that oversized cardboard cartons can be cut apart and re-shaped as new structural forms. These will provide students with creative challenges and a source for making free-standing three-dimensional forms that can become sculptures, figures, buildings, or anything else you imagine.

Experimenting with letter forms. Here's a way that familiar letter forms become integrated as art elements—lines, shapes, and spaces. Ask students to fill a 4" x 12" strip of paper with the letters of their names printed full size, in upper-case letters. Explain that all of the letters must touch so that the lines of the letter forms reach the top, sides, and bottom of the strip of paper.

If students thicken the lines of the letters a bit, they'll notice that the lines form positive shapes. The spaces between the lines become negative shapes. Students can then fill in the negative shapes with decorative line elements experimenting with different techniques to create a personal statement. They can use color to liven up their artwork. Incidentally, the completed name art-strips make beautiful borders for a display of class work. This is a handy activity for the beginning of the school year, and ideal for decorating a work folder or portfolio.

Combining writing with shapes, colors, and lines. You can select favorite quotes or ask students to write poetry to integrate writing into elegant elements of a visual composition. Invite students to arrange the words in sizes and shapes to suit the creative spirit of the words they choose. The Swiss artist, Paul Klee, inspires us with compositions that integrate written language and visual art. Many of his paintings are filled with shimmering color that captures remarkable visual relationships between the colors and the lines and shapes.

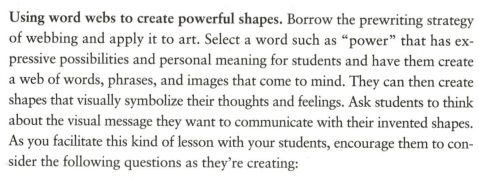

Field Notes: Teacher-To-Teacher

I believe that some lessons should be repeated several times. A recent example was a lesson we did on overlapping shapes and figures in the style of Matisse. My students kept perfecting their "finished" products. I think we were all happily surprised at the obvious progression and improvement we saw. This extra time also provided a good opportunity for students to assess themselves over time.

Sharon Nelson
Los Padres School
Salinas, California

Sometimes students grasp a concept through the pictures they create. Imagine you are studying the history of clothing in social studies, the weather in science, or character in literature. The vocabulary words and phrases from those studies can become a source for drawing shapes. For example, studying clothing of a culture or throughout history, students might come up with descriptive words to describe various articles of clothing such as hats or shoes. Then they can represent the words as shapes and put the shapes together in a composition, "what we know about the history of clothing." As they compose their pictures, ask students to think about spatial relationships and ways of creating illusions and variation through integrating other art elements.

Using word webs to create powerful shapes. Borrow the prewriting strategy of webbing and apply it to art. Select a word such as "power" that has expressive possibilities and personal meaning for students and have them create a web of words, phrases, and images that come to mind. They can then create shapes that visually symbolize their thoughts and feelings. Ask students to think about the visual message they want to communicate with their invented shapes. As you facilitate this kind of lesson with your students, encourage them to consider the following questions as they're creating:

- How do the size and form of your shapes suggest power?
- What shapes do you feel should be repeated?
- What kinds of shapes offer contrast?
- What new shapes are formed by the spaces between the shapes?
- What do you want the viewer to focus on in your picture?

Whether in pairs, small groups, or with the whole class, you and students can assess this type of learning activity by looking at criteria being studied.

It's important for students to get ongoing feedback and assessment of their work. The most important factor, though, is that students feel safe, that they trust their classroom community to be positive and constructive.

Movement and collage. You can integrate movement and art in a shape collage. I invite students to "freeze frame" moments of action or movement to capture in a composition. Decide on a topic that calls for a series of actions, such as a team sport like basketball or some other recreational activity. Ask students to work in small groups and to take turns creating appropriate physical movements in a full, expansive manner, for example, reaching out as if to catch a pass thrown by another student. Have students move slowly through the entire sequence and then ask them to "freeze" like statues when given the cue. Ask them to observe each other's shapes, and provide constructive feedback about the clarity of the shapes they make with their bodies. Sometimes students make large, quick sketches or gesture drawings to record the shapes of their bodies.

Challenge students to work as did the great French artist, Henri Matisse, to "sculpt and paint with scissors." Have them cut out large shapes to arrange in a collage. Encourage students to work directly with scissors (rather than first tracing the shape in pencil), cutting into two or three stacks of different colored construction paper at one time. The cutout figures are then separated so that there are multiple shapes to manipulate in the collage. Incidentally, the action of cutting and seeing the paper fall away from an emerging shape increases students' spontaneity and gives them direct and immediate feedback.

Field Notes: Teacher-To-Teacher

You'll be amazed at how useful a large trunk of found materials can be when you introduce the art of collage to your students. I ask friends for old issues of magazines that are good sources of visual material, like *National Geographic, Smithsonian, Travel and Leisure,* and food magazines. I recycle discarded calendars, book jackets, covers of magazines, announcements of special exhibits, museum catalogs, theater posters, and other print material. All these provide the makings of collage. I collect corrugated paper, small boxes, and save forgotten artwork to reuse in new works. What you want to gather up is a huge collection of images, textures, and kinds of paper that students can integrate or use as inspiration for other works.

—KG

"Icarus" by Henri Matisse, French, 1869-1954. Plate 8 from *Jazz*. The Metropolitan Museum of Art, Gift of Lila Acheson Wallace, 1983. [1983.1009(8)]. (C) 2000 Succession H. Matisse, Paris/Artists Rights Society (ARS), New York.

As students arrange their shapes, have them think about overlapping and connecting them to create an integrated whole. When students are satisfied with the placement of their shapes, they can glue these in place. Invite discussion about the positive shapes (the cut-out) and negative shapes (the space left by the cut-out) students have created. Matisse arranged deceptively simple shapes into compositions that are lyrical and energetic and have an almost dance-like quality. You may want to ask students to bring their collages alive by creating a movement sequence that communicates with their bodies the expressive qualities found in their completed collage.

SHOPTALK

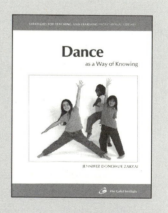

Zakkai, Jennifer Donohue. *Dance as a Way of Knowing*. Strategies for Teaching and Learning Professional Library series, The Galef Institute. York, Maine: Stenhouse Publishers, 1997.

Here is a truly upbeat and inspiring read! *Dance as a Way of Knowing* shows that being a dancer is not a requirement to integrate movement and dance into your curriculum and use it as a powerful learning tool in your classroom. With the help of detailed, easy-to-follow model lessons, you'll learn how students can use their knowledge of movement and dance to deepen and communicate what they know in all areas of the curriculum. This resource is a great starting place for incorporating this vibrant discipline into your classroom learning.

Geometric shapes and new possibilities. Apply the ideas you've learned about shapes to geometric forms. Invite students to use cylinders, cubes, or spheres to create a two-dimensional picture that appears three-dimensional. You may find it useful to refer to Chapter 3 and review some of the basic ideas about perspective. In addition, play with ideas of your own. What visual effects occur when geometric shapes seem to float in space? M.C. Escher provides many examples of the use of geometric forms that are appealing to students as they explore techniques to create volume, depth, and optical illusions in their works. To continue an exploration of geometric shapes and forms, look at examples of Cubist art, which was a style of modern art explored by Pablo Picasso and Georges Braque in the first decade of the twentieth century. Cubist artists sought to portray real subjects in a revolutionary way which resulted in simplified, flat, sometimes geometric, and abstract shapes. Often, the artists arranged and painted subjects on the canvas in such a way that viewers could see different sides of each shape simultaneously.

"Three Musicians" by Pablo Picasso. Fontainbleau, summer 1921. Oil on canvas, 6'7" x 7'3 3/4" (200.7 x 222.9 cm). The Museum of Modern Art, New York. Mrs. Simon Guggenheim Fund. Photograph ©1998 The Museum of Modern Art, New York

How Abstract Shapes Take Shape

Artists experiment. We can help students see the art in their world—encouraging them to invent new ways of expressing what they can see and integrate new ideas with existing ones. The object is to give learners the freedom to express themselves in new ways and the comfort of a supportive environment. As my nine-year-old friend Alexander once told me, "An artist is someone who can picture things. He or she can see something and picture it differently."

Picasso, perhaps the most influential artist of the twentieth century, challenged himself to put on new sets of "glasses" to create new ways of seeing the world. He once said, "Anything new, anything worth doing, can't be recognized." Picasso's body of work offers students invigorating styles and methods of working that may stimulate their imaginations and sense of daring as they look at the world and interpret what they see with different eyes. Let's look closely at Picasso's *Three Musicians*, painted in 1921. The three figures appear to be flat, invented shapes, somewhat geometric with straight and curved edges, implied lines, intricate relationships, and an interplay of colors and forms. We know Picasso studied the human figure, knew conventional ways of depicting a scene. But he made a conscious decision to experiment. He experimented with visual elements to create something startling and new, to create an abstraction of recognizable human shapes and identifiable forms. Picasso reinvented the visual language to suit his artistic goals.

Making things look abstract. To begin experimenting with abstract shapes, first ask students to put on their "realistic glasses" to see and draw some familiar object as it exists, being careful to record every detail. Then, put on a pair of "abstract glasses" to play with a different way of seeing—exaggerating one or two details. Let's try this with scissors. Look at the scissors' handle and blades. Have students draw their scissors slowly and carefully, making sure they move their pencils slowly on the paper as they continue to look at the contours and shapes of the scissors.

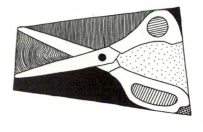

Now ask students to look at the scissors and their drawings again. What interests them and sparks their imagination? Perhaps one student likes the shape of the blades, another the way the scissors change shape when it is open and closed. Next, students put on their "abstract glasses" and imagine their scissors can stand, unsupported, in front of one of those carnival mirrors that distort and exaggerate images. First the scissors looks long, stretched out, and tall; then short and flattened; then curved in the middle. Ask students to draw what they imagine. They might draw the scissors as a series of abstract shapes scattered across the page or use different index cards to practice on first. If they don't like something they've drawn, they can go over it with a different colored pencil, but ask students not to erase. They can use colors that are not usually associated with a scissors. Finally,

have students look closely at the shapes and the ways they've portrayed this common object. They might recreate the scissors as a series of movable cut-out shapes and arrange these on a sheet of paper in a collage.

Another terrific exercise in creating abstract art is through unconventional group portraits. I encourage students to bring in photographs of family members and friends to work from. Then students use shapes, lines, and colors to stretch their imaginations and experience making whimsical, humorous, or even ironic artwork. Bring in works by artists who empower students to bend the rules, such as Marisol Escobar, the French-Venezuelan artist who combines wood with plaster to create sculptures that are biting yet humorous statements of what she views as problems in government and in her family.

The Magic of Space

Artists use space, as they do the other art elements, to communicate. Sometimes they create believable, realistic space. Or they may bend conventional ideas of space.

There will be no stopping your students once they begin examining how to use space.

There will be no stopping your students once they begin examining how to use space. Students thrive when given opportunities to explore and enlarge their art repertoire. You and your students can keep your eyes and minds open to what is around you and develop an awareness of what you can do with space. Keep looking, experimenting, and capturing what you see remembering to think of negative as well as positive space.

In the next chapter, we focus on the element of color and principles of design. Normally, color is included in discussions of the five art elements. I decided to give color its own spotlight because children find working with color so exciting and almost magical.

Chapter 5

The Element of Color and Principles of Design

An artist is a person who has a powerful imagination and skill in colors.

Santiago, age 9

Working with color provides endless opportunities for experimentation and personal expression. Color can suggest a mood, portray a season, or release a memory. We use color to make what we see seem real in our artwork by painting a sky blue, or we can startle ourselves and others by painting pink and orange trees against a green sky. Color helps us make distinctions among shapes. It seems to breathe life into art.

It's usually pleasant for us to discover that a red apple is not just red. When you ask students to look for the colors in an apple, they'll begin to see that it may have subtle touches of orange and even violet. Similarly, a green tree is not the same green as a lime green tennis ball; and a tree trunk isn't just brown—it may have tones of brown, shades of orange, tints of pink, light and dark values of color, and a variety of textures. You and your students will discover the joy of seeing color with fresh eyes as you begin mixing colors, thinking in color, and adding color to your visual vocabulary.

SHOPTALK

Zhensun, Zheng and Alice Low. *A Young Painter: The Life and Paintings of Wang Yani—China's Extraordinary Young Artist.* New York: Scholastic, 1991.

The biography of child prodigy Wang Yani is a rare book that is as much about lifelong learning, openness, and trust as it is about visual art. Yani's father is an artist who nurtures Yani's talent and stimulates her to inspire him. Each time I want to buy a present for someone, I purchase a copy of *A Young Painter* because there is so much to learn from it. You'll use this remarkable book as a resource for ideas about painting and to understand the daily life and customs of Chinese society. Yani's own brush paintings and an introduction to techniques and the art of Chinese painting encourage students to try their own paintings. A teaching guide and videotape may be borrowed from the publisher, free of charge.

One Color Leads to Another

What do your students already know about color? What colors do they like using best? Have any students mixed colors before? As always, starting with students' sharing what they know and would like to learn more about is best. After students share their color experiences, tell them they'll be learning how to mix colors to make other fabulous colors. They'll hypothesize about what they'll produce when they mix colors together. But, first, they'll need to expand their color vocabulary.

The primary colors. The *primary* colors are red, yellow and blue. One primary combined with another leads to *secondary* colors, which make up the colors in the visual spectrum. Reading about color is a bit like reading about the sound of a meadowlark. The descriptions on the next couple of pages will have substantially more meaning for you and your students if you can experience the actual making of a color wheel. Creating a color wheel with students will give them a visual reference and the security to create a range of exciting colors. When starting color-mixing activities, tempera or acrylic paints work best.

The secondary colors. Secondary colors are made by mixing two primary colors. While color perception is to some extent subjective, it is generally accepted that blue and yellow make green, yellow and red make orange, and red and blue make violet. Thus green, orange, and violet are considered the secondary colors and fall between the primary colors on the color wheel.

Tertiary colors. We make *tertiary* colors by mixing a primary color with a secondary color. The six tertiary colors so created will be yellow-orange, yellow-green, blue-green, blue-violet, red-violet, and red-orange. Each tertiary color is a combination of the two that were mixed to create it. (See wheel below.)

Warm, cool, harmonious, and contrasting colors. Colors are grouped together to form color families. Generally, *warm* colors range from yellows to red-violet on the wheel and make us think of setting suns and sunny dispositions. The family of cool colors includes a range from yellow-green to red-violet. *Cool* colors can be used to create more sober feelings or quiet environments in a work of art. *Harmonious* colors are generally alike or near one another on the color wheel, such as, yellow, orange, yellow-orange, and red-orange. *Contrasting* colors are those that fall opposite one another on the color wheel, like red and green, blue and orange, or yellow and violet. Contrasting colors, when used together, create vibrant effects.

Neutrals, lights, and darks. When contrasting colors are mixed they become muted, what I refer to as "the muds," or *neutrals*. Neutral colors are used to add shadowy effects or to tame the brightness of colors in a work of art. Students can mix different proportions of either primary or contrasting colors to create browns, tans, and maroons. Creating these neutral colors is a little like cooking because what students get depends on the recipe they develop.

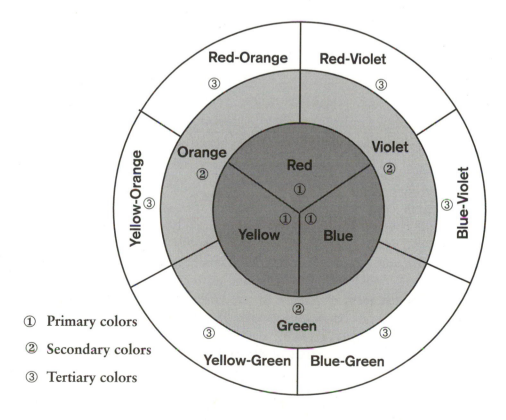

① Primary colors

② Secondary colors

③ Tertiary colors

Creating tints and shades. *Tints* of a color are made by adding white, and *shades* of a color are created by adding black. Depending on the degree of white or black you add to any color, you'll change the lightness and darkness of a color.

Black and white are not included in color charts or wheels because they aren't colors that are seen in the rainbow. Theoretically, black is the absence of all light, so the darkest value is pure black. Pure white is the absence of all color. Putting white and black right next to each other provides the greatest degree of contrast.

It's useful for students to know how to use black and white to create special effects or accents in their work.

Review these points as you and students mix colors.

- Primary colors exist as "pure" red, yellow, and blue.
- Secondary colors can be created by mixing two primary colors half-and-half. For example, half red and half yellow give you orange.
- Tertiary colors can be created by making a mixture of 75 percent of a primary color and 25 percent of a secondary color; so, for example, 75 percent of red plus 25 percent of yellow-orange give you red-orange. By changing the percentages of the two colors mixed, you can create variations of a color. For example, by mixing 25 percent of red with 75 percent yellow-orange, you'll create an orange-yellow that is more intensely orange.

Field Notes: Teacher-To-Teacher

I like to set aside a couple of periods for students to create a personal color wheel. Students benefit a great deal from experimenting and mixing their own colors. I know our time is well spent when I see how engaged and delighted students are in what they're learning. I use the occasion to demonstrate fundamental lessons in using different kinds of paint and watercolor techniques, and I show students how to care for materials and their workspaces. I'm always amazed that students consider their color wheels a mark of personal accomplishment and see these as a way of showing they have expertise.

–KG

Basic Colors

Primary Colors: Red, Yellow, Blue
Primary colors are pure colors and can't be produced from mixing other colors.

Secondary Colors: Orange, Green, Violet
Mixing two primary colors in equal amounts yields the secondary colors.

Tertiary Colors: Red-Orange, Yellow-Orange, Yellow-Green, Blue-Green, Red-Violet, Blue-Violet
Mixing a secondary color with individual primary colors creates tertiary colors.

Neutral Colors: Browns, Tans, Grays, and Maroons
Mixing together all the primary colors or pairs of contrasting colors provides neutral colors.

Light and Dark Colors: Tints, and Shades
Various amounts of white or black added to any color create tints and shades.

All proportions are approximate, and the results will vary with the color medium. Experimenting is half the fun.

In the beginning, students enjoy using tempera or acrylic paint for color-mixing lessons because they can gain more control over the results. These are less likely to "bleed" or fade as much as watercolors do. I usually have scrap paper for trying out colors and provide reusable white plastic picnic plates for palettes so that students can see what emerges. Once they have the knack of mixing tempera or acrylic paint, move on to opaque watercolors. You can also try color mixing with crayons, oil pastels, or colored pencils to see the effects of layering and blending colors.

Explore Color-Mixing Projects

There are a number of ways to practice mixing color. You may prefer an intuitive color-mixing strategy to let students discover their own recipes for creating new colors. Or you may prefer a systematic approach. For the latter, try the following suggestions.

Mix food coloring and water. Fill a jar with water and add food coloring a drop at a time, watching the dyes slowly blend to make new colors. Try different combinations and record observations on a sheet of paper. For example, one drop of red and two drops of yellow; one drop of red and three drops of blue, and so on. Predict what will happen and then check it out. Experiment with different proportions. The same procedures can be tried with watercolors.

Mix food coloring and milk. Laurine DiRocco, an early childhood teacher and visual artist from Los Angeles, California, gathers students around a table where she has stacks of white bread, a toaster, several small containers filled with milk, food-coloring, eye droppers, and clean paint brushes. Her students create "colored milk," paint the mixture on bread, and toast the bread to set their color designs. They then cheer, clap, and display the results.

Mix wax crayon or oil pastels to create a plaid pattern. This is actually a type of color layering that will enhance your students' understanding of color mixing and the technique of layering and blending colors. Use a stack of newspaper to cushion the drawing paper, to make easier the application of crayons or oil pastels. On a sheet of white paper, evenly lay down one-inch wide vertical stripes of red, yellow, and blue next to each other. Then layer horizontal stripes of the same colors over the vertical colors. The secondary colors will emerge with a little careful blending. To get more evenly blended colors, lay down white and light colors first and put darker ones next to them before blending. Fingers work best for blending colors because the natural oils in our skin interact nicely with the oil-based pastels and wax-based crayons. Use light pressure when blending so that you don't tear the paper or rub off all the color. Use tissues to clean fingers and the tips of the oil pastels.

Mix new colors with colored pencils to practice hatching and crosshatching. Blend colors with your fingers as you build up hatching and crosshatching layers with colored pencils. Artist David Hockney provides excellent models for seeing the versatility you can get from colored pencils. Some types of colored pencils can be moistened to achieve a watercolor effect.

Expressing Yourself in Color

It's time to express ourselves in color. Using a specific color family and experimenting with combinations based on the color wheel, students can express how they feel, define a season, or represent a memory. They'll no doubt be tempted to use every color of the rainbow, but ask them to use a little restraint. A limited color palette forces us to be self-disciplined, to make creative choices and explore dynamics that we might not otherwise try. In Picasso's words, "Forcing yourself to use restricted means is the sort of restraint that liberates invention. It obliges you to make a kind of progress that you can't even imagine in advance."

Experimenting with tints and shades. Mixing tints and shades will add to students' repertoire of tools for creating different visual effects and adding interest to their artwork. For this lesson, you'll need white, black, and one other color. Mix tints by adding increasing amounts of white paint to the color and paint swatches that represent the range from light to dark. Mix shades by adding increasing amounts of black to the color and paint swatches that represent the range from dark to light. Then pick the best ones that represent an even progression towards the middle range and cut into tiles. These can be glued on white paper to create a useful reference chart.

A limited color palette forces us to be self-disciplined, to make creative choices, and explore dynamics that we might not otherwise try.

| Lightest Tints | Lighter | Light | Dark Shades | Darker | Darkest |

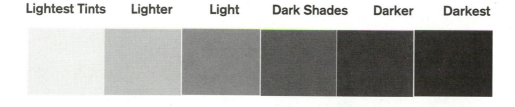

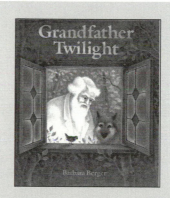

SHOPTALK

Berger, Barbara. *Grandfather Twilight.* New York: Philomel Books, 1984.

Berger's lovely story will enchant students, and her illustrations will help them see how an artist uses color to convey mood and meaning. Grandfather Twilight brings the different tints and shades of twilight to the sky as he walks through the woods to the ocean and gently gives the moon up to the sky. Berger's choices of hues of pink, peach, blue, purple, green, and yellow will, no doubt, give students their own ideas about how they might use color in their own paintings.

Playing with color

It's a good idea to have students experiment and explore with color in a series of paintings. A trip outside to look at cloud formations and the sky at various times of the day may help students see different tints and shades in nature. Looking at the way different artists have dealt with tints and shades in their works will also provide techniques to consider.

Ask students to create a series of paintings using cool and warm colors. Students can divide a large sheet of painting paper into interesting shapes for painting. For example, they can lightly pencil in a series of geometric shapes, a pattern of thick and thin stripes, or outlines of objects. Tessellations work nicely if you want to integrate math with the painting project.

As noted earlier, tempera and acrylic paint are good for students to begin with because the thick consistency and opaque quality make these easier to use than watercolors. However, watercolor is a favorite medium, and with a little practice and some helpful hints, you can help students produce watercolors that keep their vibrant, fresh colors. Teachers often ask for guidance when they bring watercolors into the classroom for everyday use, so here are five general guidelines and some suggested techniques that you can explore with your students.

General Guidelines for Working with Watercolor

- Stroke paint on with your brush, don't scrub it in.
- Keep the colors looking fresh and moist by keeping your brush and water clean.
- Load the brush with plenty of color because the paint tends to fade when it dries.
- Try to use paper with "tooth" or texture to hold the watercolor.
- Use less water for more saturated color.

Exploring Watercolor Techniques

Students must try out different techniques before feeling confident and becoming proficient in using watercolors. Here are some techniques that have worked well with my students.

- **Wash on dry paper.** Load the brush with paint and stroke the brush across the top of the paper. Use water sparingly to draw the color down to make a transparent wash.
- **Wet on wet.** Moisten the paper lightly with a sponge or brush, load the brush with color, and apply while the paper is still wet.
- **Overpainting.** Paint lines, shapes, images, details, and other colors over dry areas that have already been painted with lighter colors.
- **Dry brush.** Load the brush with color, remove excess moisture from it with a paper towel, and pull the brush across the surface of the paper for textured effects.
- **Pulling.** Load the brush with color and pull the brush toward or away from you on a wet or dry surface.
- **Rolling.** Load the brush with color and use a rolling motion, holding the brush sideways, to move the brush across a wet or dry surface.
- **Printing.** Load a small damp sponge with color and use it to print on a dry or wet surface.
- **Dotting.** Load a stiff bristle brush with color and "dot" on a wet or dry surface.
- **Using negative white space.** Let the white of the paper play a part in your color thinking.

Field Notes: Teacher-To-Teacher

In a studio painting class many years ago, I had the good fortune to have as an instructor the painter William Brice who gave me advice I've always remembered. I was painting away on a large still-life composition using a cool, quiet palette of subtle tints and shades. I had been struggling with this assignment for several days when Brice stopped in front of my work, considered it with me, and finally said in his rather ironic way, "You know, your painting is all about whisper, whisper, whisper. Every now and again, you need a pow," and while he spoke he gestured toward my painting with emphatic stabs at the places on the canvas where he thought I should add "pow." I like to remind students that subtle paintings can have an element of surprise, or a pow that makes the quietness even more intense.

–KG

Creating Paintings Together

After your students develop some comfort and skill on their own with the elements of art, it's a nice idea to provide them with opportunities to collaborate on a small mural or some form of group painting. I like to begin with a circular format because it presents an easy way for students to develop their intuition about ways to create a work that is well-balanced, unified, and visually pleasing in preparation for thinking about the principles of design. Cut large sheets of butcher or craft paper into 24-inch circles and invite students to think about a theme such as celebration. Ask students to use their senses to imagine how they would paint shapes and colors to represent their feelings about a celebration. Ask them to agree on one or two major ideas they want to express through their group painting, applying what they know about color, shape, and line.

Before students begin painting, have a conversation about work habits to help them focus on ways they can collaborate and cooperate. I like to talk about respecting individual artistic decisions while keeping in mind the creative decisions to which the group has agreed. I ask students to

• honor the work space and painting of group members
• paint up to, but not through someone else's work

- share ideas and tools
- move all around the circle to assess the emerging mural
- evaluate their personal contributions to the group process by looking back at how they followed the criteria we set out with.

Students involved in group art projects learn to rely on, cooperate, and respect each other, thus gaining a sense of security as artists. Students also start to look to the world to participate, to learn, to receive, and to give. There are other painting projects that involve group participation and collaboration that you may want to try. Worthy projects include murals and posters to illustrate events that students are learning about in literature, to illustrate important points in history or social studies, and to depict family and school gatherings. You'll want to lead up to those projects by making sure that all students have opportunities to understand the concepts behind the art elements and design principles and to develop the aesthetic knowledge and skills that will allow them use their visual vocabulary as creative tools.

Students involved in group art projects learn to rely on, cooperate, and respect each other, thus gaining a sense of security as artists.

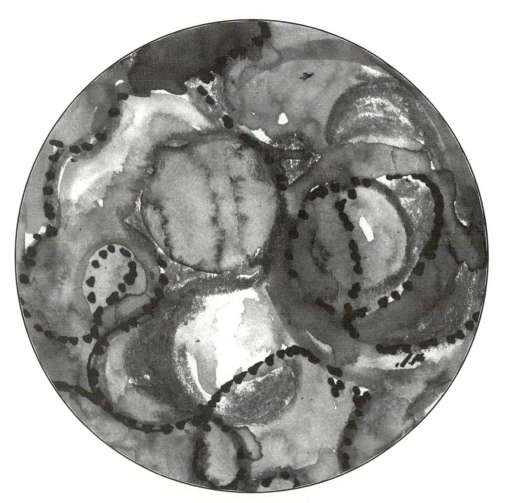

DIALOGUE

What connections between color mixing and math and science can I help students discover?

_____

_____

Think about how color is used to express ideas in drama.

_____

_____

What art books, postcards, and other resources can I make available to help children see how artists use color?

_____

_____

Exploring the Principles of Design

In the lessons and projects you've already tried, you've undoubtedly noticed that students tend to create compositions even when they are experimenting with an individual art element. Even without realizing it—and even when concentrating on a single element—students make aesthetic decisions based on the principles of design.

It's helpful when students develop understanding of the design choices they can make when creating a composition. Knowledge of the principles of design as organizational tools for obtaining a look of unity in their work deepens students' intuitive sense of aesthetic qualities and is empowering. Let's explore the principles of design known as balance, rhythm, repetition, pattern, contrasts, theme, variation, and dominance. In this way, you and your students will acquire a working vocabulary to be able to talk about your creative choices.

Balance

Balance occurs when objects or art elements are placed in such a way as to produce a sense of equilibrium in a composition or design. Artists think about balance as either *formal* or *informal*. Students understand the basic idea of formal, or symmetrical balance, when they create mirror images. Simply put, formal balance means that objects or art elements are organized on both sides of a real or implied center line. Ask students to fold a piece of paper in half to form a center fold. Invite them to paint shapes on one side of the paper. Then while the paint is still moist, ask them to re-fold the paper to transfer the design to the unpainted side.

Radial balance is also symmetrical. This formal principle of balance can be achieved by placing shapes and lines in four equally spaced places emanating from a central point. Demonstrate radial balance for students by folding a square piece of paper in fourths. Place an "x" or "plus" to mark the center point. Starting from that center point, draw a shape or lines in one of the quarter sections. Repeat the image in each of the other quarter sections. A

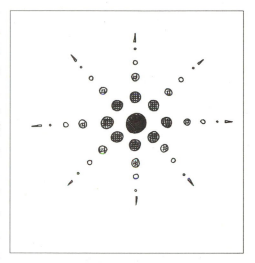

circular format is another simple way to demonstrate the design principle of radial balance by placing objects at equal distance from the center of the circle. For examples of radial balance, students can look at drawings of sun motifs; flowers, such as daisies; and designs in kaleidoscopes.

Field Notes: Teacher-To-Teacher

Brian, a fourth-grader, once told me that he had two favorite activities in my classroom—one was painting like an artist of his choice and the second was reading about the artist as a "real person." I've always had information about art and artists in my classroom library that includes the whole spectrum of world art and culture—from magazines to histories, biographies, short stories, and picture books. Many times I've found that women artists are overlooked. I make sure to supplement where necessary to create a balance. I've discovered that children make all kinds of connections to their own lives through reading and raise interesting questions that make them eager to learn more.

—KG

Informal, *or asymmetrical* balance, occurs when equilibrium is created even when objects on both sides of a center line are not equal in size. We manipulate the use and placement of colors, shapes, and lines to create a sense of implied balance.

Using Rhythm, Repetition, and Pattern

Textile designs make use of *rhythm*, *repetition*, and *pattern*. Display some fabrics or a book of wallpaper samples that clearly demonstrate these design principles. Colors flowing through a painting can create rhythm as well as pattern. The positioning of shapes can make your eyes move through a painting. Marc Chagall's painting, *Birthday, 1915*, is an example: two figures seem weightless as their shapes create an upward rhythmic movement. Ask students to create regular and irregular pattern and rhythm by repeating lines, shapes, textures, or colors.

"Birthday, 1915" by Marc Chagall. Oil on cardboard, 31 3/4" x 39" 1/4" The Museum of Modern Art, New York. Acquired through the Lillie P. Bliss Bequest. Photograph ©1999 The Museum of Modern Art, New York. (C) 2000 Artists Rights Society (ARS), New York/ADAGP, Paris.

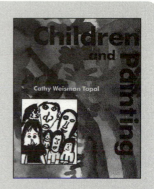

SHOPTALK

Topal, Cathy Weisman. *Children and Painting*. Worcester, Massachusetts: Davis Publications, 1992.

Whether you are just getting started or well on your way to integrating painting across the curriculum in your classroom, here is a marvelous resource for you and your students. Weisman provides warm-up exercises to help develop understanding and confidence about the art elements and basic design principles. She suggests thematic approaches to painting and ways to help students develop basic painting techniques and approaches. You'll find step-by-step guidance in facilitating students' awareness of fine art as well as questions to help stimulate their thinking about painting.

Cathy Weisman Topal, author of *Children and Painting*, offers suggestions for helping students do this. She invites them to choose an art element, such as line or shape, and follow its use as a design principle in painting. Topal's book is a great resource for your own professional library.

Contrast, Theme and Variation, and Dominance

As artists, we work with a variety of design principles to express our ideas. For example, we arrrange shapes, lines, color, or other elements of art to create interesting contrasts. The contrasts may take the form of opposites: a delicate line next to a bold one, or red opposite green. We may develop theme and variation in our work by repeating and varying a shape. Sometimes we draw attention to an important or powerful part of a picture by applying the principle of dominance. This means the viewer's eyes are drawn to a dominant part of the work. Dominance can be achieved through the placement of art elements such as color or shape, or use of design principles like rhythm or repetition.

Unity

Through work with the art elements, you and your students will begin to have an awareness of what makes a picture seem whole, or unified. For example, in Van Gogh's *Starry Night,* his use of color, brush strokes, and line create unified swirling patterns that draw your eyes to the starry sky. (See page 108.)

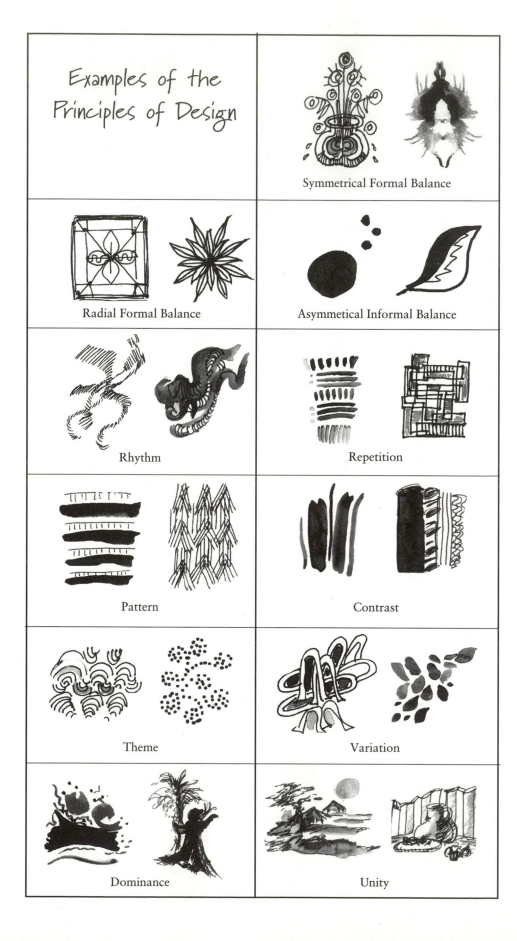

Examples of the Principles of Design

Symmetrical Formal Balance

Radial Formal Balance

Asymmetical Informal Balance

Rhythm

Repetition

Pattern

Contrast

Theme

Variation

Dominance

Unity

Making Creative Choices

Help students expand and deepen their understanding of the principles of design by putting what they've learned into regular practice in drawings, paintings, designs, story illustrations, collages, graphic works, and other forms of art expression. Guide students to decide on their creative and artistic intentions and challenge them to use a variety of devices to create works that are aesthetically pleasing. Continue to encourage them to extend the skills they have developed, deepening their understanding of design principles.

For example, help students apply different ways to achieve balance in their works. See what your students come up with in compositions when they are asked to choose elements of art and principles of design that work within these four basic areas of balance:

- Formal, symmetrically balanced work.
- Formal, radial balance created by placing elements so that the eyes focus on the center of the composition, and then move gradually to the outer edges of the picture surface (a large white paper plate can serve as a template for a circular composition.)

- Formal balance with a triangular arrangement in which the art elements move the eyes upward toward an apex (this is a familiar principle in paintings having a spiritual focus).
- Informal balance using contrasting shapes and colors, in which arrangement of the art elements will create the asymmetrical balance.

A disciplined approach to practicing techniques will ultimately bring out the creativity and very best intentions in all students. There is no "one way" to solve a design problem, and this fact gives students myriad opportunities to find out new things about themselves as creative problem solvers. In making art, students are always involved in a process of ongoing assessment that informs them about their progress and helps you the teacher make decisions about your teaching.

Let's look at the next chapter to become familiar with strategies and tools for assessing and reflecting on the process and products of art so that students are able to evaluate their own intentions and how well they achieve them.

Chapter 6

Integrating Art, Learning, and Assessment

I have learned that I am an excellent artist. People remember me and know what I'm learning through my art.

Ulisis, age 10

So many times I'm struck by the artwork of a particular student, astonished by the depth of a group discussion about the merits of surrealist art, and surprised as children ask to give up their recess time to work on an art project. After studying Rene Magritte and Joan Miro, ten-year-old Lily created her amazing visual and verbal impression of shapes below.

"Everything comes away floating in the sky. The color changes and moves. If you squint your eyes you can see the balls come and float away. They go in and out and in and out."

Lily, age 10

Why do our students like art? What are they learning? What sense of self-discipline, personal accomplishment, and successes are they feeling? How does that transfer into other areas of the curriculum? Assessment can help answer those questions as well as tell you what students are willing and able to do when they are highly engaged in their work. (See *Assessment in Art Education* by Donna Kay Beattie on page 71.)

Ten-year-old Lily, whose visual and verbal skills are represented on page 103, arrived at this stage of maturity and skill through a process that included learning about art principles, setting goals for herself in gaining command over these principles, making art, and assessing her process with every piece she created.

We assess both to learn and to teach. Ongoing assessment in visual arts helps students and teachers become aware of and understand the creative- and critical-thinking processes and intuitive decisions that go into making a work of art. Assessment provides feedback about the quality of learning experiences. Used effectively, it shapes the way students and teachers thrive in a trusting classroom environment. Viewed this way, assessment is integrated with every interaction in the classroom and becomes part of a continuous cycle of learning that benefits both students and teachers.

A Cycle of Learning and Assessment
In *Different Ways of Knowing* curriculum modules, this continuous cycle of learning and assessment is represented in three parts. They are known as *Coming To Know: The Process of Learning*; *Showing You Know: The Products of Learning*; and *Knowing You Know: Reflections*.

One way to get started documenting how and what children are learning is by using the following *Different Ways of Knowing* kidwatching forms. You'll find that as you think through the art projects you assign, and the concepts, content, and skills you wish students to learn, you'll adapt and design assessments to get at questions such as, "What do my students already know?" "What will the assessment tell me about my students' needs?" "What next steps will my students and I need to take together?"

Keep in mind that continuous assessment will help you look at the full spectrum of students' understandings, interests, and expectations. In this chapter we'll explore

- assessment tools such as portfolios, learning logs, journals, sketchbooks, anecdotal records, class critiques, discussions, and conversations
- how teachers use these tools in their classrooms
- the use of assessment data to guide you in reaching your professional goals for teaching to high standards and continuous learning for all students.

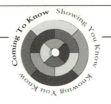

STUDENT'S NAME

Coming To Know
The Process of Learning

DATE	LEARNING EVENT	ENGAGEMENT • pleasure and involvement • perseverance • risk-taking • responsibility	COLLABORATION • thoughts expressed • openness to feedback • use of input • group work	FLEXIBILITY • modalities used • problem-solving strategies • revision strategies

Different Ways of Knowing © 1994, 1996 The Galef Institute

Kidwatching Form **1**

STUDENT'S NAME

Showing You Know
The Products of Learning

DATE	LEARNING EVENT	UNDERSTANDING CONTENT • verbal and nonverbal expressions of main idea	CONVENTIONS AND FORMS • first uses of conventions • practiced use of conventions	PRESENTATION • clarity • detail • focus • purpose • voice

Different Ways of Knowing © 1994, 1996 The Galef Institute

Kidwatching Form **2**

STUDENT'S NAME

Knowing You Know
Reflections

The essence of education may well be the ability to look back on the learning experience and evaluate what worked and why, and what didn't work and why. Self-reflection—thinking about learning—helps students discover what they have learned, how they learned it, and what they should do next to extend and refine their learning. Please duplicate the *Learning About My Learning* student self-reflection form (on the other side of this form) and use it whenever you feel it is appropriate. Your students' self-reflections will help you plan instruction and create curriculum that will best support them.

DATE	LEARNING EVENT	WHERE WE'VE BEEN • the learner's plan for learning • the learner's strengths	WHERE WE GO NEXT • the learner's needs

Different Ways of Knowing © 1994, 1996 The Galef Institute

Kidwatching Form **3**

Learning About My Learning

STUDENT'S NAME	DATE

WHAT I CAN DO

WHAT I WANT TO DO

WHAT I KNOW

WHAT I WANT TO KNOW

WHAT I WILL DO NEXT

Different Ways of Knowing © 1994, 1996 The Galef Institute

Kidwatching Form **4**

SHOPTALK

Bird, Lois. *Assessment: Continuous Learning.*
Strategies for Teaching and Learning Professional
Library series, The Galef Institute. York, Maine:
Stenhouse Publishers, 1995.

Here's a guide that provides a backbone for
understanding the integral role of learning and assessment. Bird
defines assessment as a continuous process for all learners—students,
teachers, and parents. She describes ways in which we can empower
each other as lifelong learners. You'll find that Bird's Six Defining
Principles of Authentic Assessment serve as benchmarks for marking
your progress as a professional who is always learning.

*We learn alongside
our students.*

A Classroom of Active, Responsive Learners

Let's take a peek into Jennifer Uecker's second grade class at Cohasset
Elementary School in Van Nuys, California, to get a glimpse of responsive
teaching and learning. Uecker decided to integrate art more fully into her classroom because she felt this would motivate all students and engage them in rigorous academic learning. Uecker also wanted to stimulate children's multiple
intelligences (Gardner 1983) as a way to reach more of her students. She
thought that regular inclusion of visual arts would be a good starting point.

Uecker set her goals to include visual arts regularly in her class with a little
trepidation because she had no formal training in art or art history. But she
had enjoyed the one art class she had taken in high school and had a box of
leftover art supplies and materials. She had already observed her students in
other learning activities, and felt they would be responsive to finding different ways of expressing themselves. To prepare, Uecker looked through some
art books to refresh her memory about art techniques and skills. Then she
started gathering books and resources that would help her students learn
about the lives of famous artists. Among these was Mike Venezia's *Getting To
Know the World's Greatest Artists* series (1988).

Uecker began facilitating a course of study around well-known artists and their
works. She also taught students about the elements of art and the principles of
design to help them create their own work and understand the work of others.
As Uecker explains, "I learn alongside my students. I assess my choice of instructional strategies and specific content while I develop an understanding of
what my students are able to do. I also think about appropriate challenges for
individuals as well as for groups of students." Uecker engages students in

conversations about their art as they're working, observes their progress, and asks them to complete self-reflections and student evaluations once they've completed a painting. Students comment on what they like, what they've learned, how they learned, and how they view their work. This routine gives Uecker an overall picture of what students know and are able to do.

In anticipation of a field trip to the Norton Simon Museum in Pasadena, California, where students would see some "real" art of Van Gogh, Picasso, and Degas, Uecker and her students focused on a study of Vincent Van Gogh. Studying his life and work helped their understanding of what constitutes a master artist. Students participated in a series of five half-hour afternoon sessions to develop understanding of the use of color to express emotion and to explore the design principles in composition. The students read Mike Venezia's *Van Gogh* from the *Getting To Know the World's Greatest Artists* series to make connections to language arts and reading. Uecker provided other resources for further research, guided students in observing and discussing reproductions of some of Van Gogh's works, and gave students opportunities to practice color-mixing techniques. Uecker asked students to point out what they saw in Van Gogh's works, and questioned them about visual characteristics they noticed that were similar to effects they wanted to achieve in their own work. Students talked about the perspective and odd angles of the furniture in the painting *Bedroom at Arles*, 1888 (see page 167), and discussed the visual impact, use of

"The Starry Night" by Vincent Van Gogh, 1889. Oil on canvas, 1888, 29 x 36-1/4", The Museum of Modern Art, New York. Acquired through the Lillie P. Bliss Bequest. Photograph ©1998, The Museum of Modern Art, New York.

By Jessica, age 6

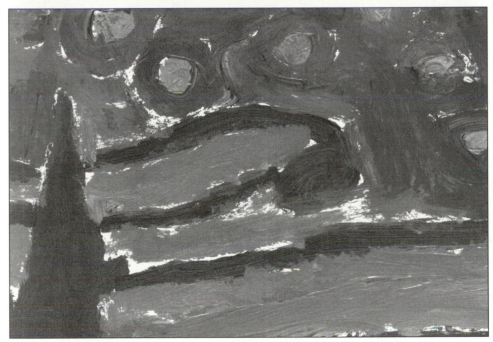

By Levom, age 7

brush strokes, and placement of objects in *The Starry Night*, 1889. Uecker asked her students to use *The Starry Night* and what they had learned about Van Gogh as a source for their own interpretations of a night painting. Her goal was to have students demonstrate skills of color-mixing with a limited palette of colors, while gaining technical expertise and comfort with acrylic paint and brush techniques. She also wanted students to apply what they learned about creating a balanced composition, and she looked for a synthesis of their learning in their paintings.

Throughout this learning process, Uecker kidwatches, using adaptations of the *Coming To Know* and *Showing You Know* forms to get at specific assessment goals she has in mind. Her purpose for observing students in the color-mixing phase of the project is to assess their understanding of color theory and their technical color-mixing skills. She and her students want to see how well they're able to create shades, tints, and expressive visual qualities with yellow, white, black, and blue acrylic paint. They're interested in developing technical skill, craftsmanship, creativity, and artistic flexibility. As students begin to create their own paintings, Uecker guides them to focus on assessing

- how well they plan ahead for their painting
- what goes into preparing the initial sketch
- what revisions they make
- what visual balance they will create through the placement of objects and colors
- how creative they will be within the context of "working like Van Gogh."

She does this often by beginning her own painting and modeling the process. Uecker thinks out loud, then poses questions about her work. Quite often she doesn't finish her picture, creating just enough to get the children started on their own.

As you picture Uecker and her students working together in their classroom, you can see that the focus on Van Gogh integrates the making and thinking of art with assessment, learning, and teaching. Learning about art at this point is her primary focus, but several learning goals are integrated in the process. The students express themselves nonverbally through their art and verbally in their discussions and written comments. Uecker can observe how well they take risks, persevere, collaborate, take responsibility for their own learning, and fulfill the criteria she has set for color-mixing and creating a balanced and unified picture.

Knowing what you want to teach and assess and establishing standards of achievement for each part of the learning event help you develop appropriate criteria and rubrics. Remember that you don't have to assess everything at once. Assessment occurs over time, and you can start by focusing on those areas which are priorities.

I like to plan backwards, figuring out what I want students to learn as a way of planning for what students need. This way, you can use a variety of assessment techniques and continually assess as students learn. Continuous assessment informs us where students are in the learning process and enables us to modify the teaching and learning journey. As you plan to integrate assessment with learning, ask yourself the following *Dialogue* questions.

DIALOGUE

What do my students need to know (for example, about art elements, design principles, or historic and cultural themes in art)?

_____

_____

_____

What specific skills, facts, and generalizations do they already know? What technical skills will they acquire?

_____

_____

_____

What essential procedures or processes will be important for students to understand? Will there be exceptions?

_____

_____

What self-reflection will help students develop personal learning goals?

_____

_____

What new interests might students have about the topic they've studied?

_____

_____

How will I guide students to make connections about themselves as creative learners and problem solvers?

_____

_____

S H O P T A L K

Wolf, Dennie Palmer and Nancy Pistone. *Taking Full Measure: Rethinking Assessment Through the Arts.* New York: College Entrance Examination Board, 1991.

This valuable book describes assessment projects in photography, dance, drama, music, and the visual arts; and it provides new insights about assessing the arts to guide teaching and learning in all classrooms. *Taking Full Measure* looks at how art teachers use multiple strategies such as checklists, portfolios, interviews, and class critiques to enhance their students' thinking skills and develop students' ability to become thoughtful critics of their own work. Wolf and Pistone make five assumptions about the effectiveness of assessment in the arts:

- Students and teachers openly discuss expectations for excellence and reaching high standards in learning.
- Students and teachers evaluate by looking at a range of expressive qualities in a piece, not at a single dimension.
- Students take part in self-assessment that helps them understand and learn about their work.
- Teachers and students use different forms of assessment to examine individual and group performances.
- Assessment is ongoing and continuous, and gives students opportunities to reflect on and use constructive criticism in their work.

The author's assessment strategies work not only for art teachers, but for generalists as well.

Assessment Strategies

When I stop to think about the enormous range of assessment strategies we can use to develop understanding about how students learn, I think about being an investigative reporter: digging for essential evidence and using multiple methods and tools—in this case, portfolios, learning logs, journals, sketchbooks, anecdotal records, interviews, audiotapes, photographs, and written documents. My goal is to piece together a comprehensive story about how students have performed and demonstrated their understanding. Documenting the story of learning is a complex task. We want to manage assessment as part of the general flow of teaching and learning. Ultimately, assessment empowers students to understand themselves as learners. Here are some tried and true assessment strategies that have worked for me and other teachers. Adapt these strategies and add your own to meet the particular needs of your students.

Portfolios

Portfolios show what students learn over time. There is no one right way to put together a portfolio; still you must decide on your purpose and how you and your students will manage the process. Ask yourself questions like these:

- Who is the audience for the portfolio?
- Will you use the portfolio as an accountability and assessment strategy?
- What kind of work will you ask students to submit?
- What will you and your students do with the information you derive from reviewing the contents of the portfolios?

What has worked best for me is a student portfolio that contains

- specific learning goals
- a list of concepts, skills, and techniques to be learned
- a list of problems to be solved
- examples of work that show growth, development, and achievement over time.

Here are working sketches that fourth grader Sam chose to put in his portfolio as part of his study of animals. He chose them because he felt they demonstrated his mastery of pencil and pen techniques.

Assessment empowers students to understand themselves as learners.

Having students work on a "mini-portfolio" is a good way to test this learning tool. Perhaps the portfolio will demonstrate children's learning of a specific art element or unit of study. Here's one way to organize a mini-portfolio. As always, adapt it to fit the needs of your students. Also, as you become more knowledgeable about what students are able to do, invite them to take part in developing a scoring rubric that makes careful distinctions among beginning, average, highly proficient, and exemplary work.

To the Student: What To Include in Your Mini-Portfolio

1. Letter of Introduction
Introduce yourself, share your learning goals and what you want viewers to know about you as an artist and learner.

2. Table of Contents
Write down how your portfolio is organized, or make a list of what you are including.

3. Include five examples of artwork, numbered and dated on the back:
- one written reflection about your "best" artwork and why you chose it
- one written reflection about your "hardest" artwork and what made it difficult
- two homework projects showing that you researched how visual art elements are used in everyday life or by famous artists
- one example of work that shows you know how to use art to show what you have learned in math, science, reading, or writing.

3. Closing Letter
Evaluate yourself by telling what you have accomplished, how you feel about what you've learned, and what you want to do next.

If students are working on a group project, you can ask them to keep a group portfolio. A collection of brainstorms, beginning sketches, drafts of plans, research, worksheets or learning logs showing roles and responsibilities, and self-evaluations of the group endeavor hold students accountable and help them focus on working creatively and interdependently to complete a final project.

Ultimately, you and students can work together to decide on the purpose for your porfolios. Make a list of what work to include, and plan how to assess the work. Portfolios also serve as an effective tool for informing parents about what students have learned and what they'll learn next. Julie Flanagan of Anderson School in Lawndale, California, periodically asks her fourth graders to take examples of work from their portfolios to share with family members. The students talk with their families about the goals of specific lessons and help them experience different ways of using art. Flanagan has found that students enjoy using the strategies they've learned in school, like brainstorming, to show their families what they know. In the teaching of others, there is always learning.

Journals and Sketchbooks

Both journals and sketchbooks are learning tools that help students capture and expand on their thinking and learning, and, in so doing, help teachers learn from their students. Journals, sometimes referred to as learning logs, are most commonly used for written notes, whereas sketchbooks have both words and pictures. I've found that journals and sketchbooks are terrific storehouses of information that help students keep visual records of their ideas, observations, notes, experiences, problem-solving strategies, reflections, and responses to questions.

Journals can be specific to a particular project or open-ended to include thoughts and observations about art experiences during the school year. The entries can help you assess students' understanding of concepts, content, and connections to other subjects as well as provide information about what students like and would like to continue doing. I like to set up five or ten minutes daily for writing in journals. Many times, students enjoy taking their journals home to continue writing. In these cases, I usually request they keep them out only overnight so we can have access to them in class each day.

If you're using sketchbooks, ask students to divide the pages in half vertically, using one side for sketches, articles, and collected images, and the other half for reflections and notes on new ideas and commentaries about their entries. Also consider having a response page for comments from you, parents, and other students. I usually ask students to include newspaper or magazine clippings, favorite images, or announcements about community art activities that interest them. Students and I then confer once a month to review and assess their entries according to criteria we have agreed upon. For example, students comb the newspaper for everything they can find about naturalists, ballet, advertising, or cartoonists.

Then I set up informal conferences with students. You can meet with small groups or set up a rotation to stagger the conferences to make the process manageable. Conferencing about sketchbook and journal entries helps give students guidance about what to include and allows you to be explicit about your expectations. A checklist can help students assess the content, form, and presentation of their entries. Here's an example of what I like students to include in their sketchbooks.

A Sketchbook Checklist

Contents

- Date and description of each assignment or project
- Drawings to clarify ideas and thinking
- Written comments—feelings about each assignment

Strategies and Ideas

- List of ideas, strategies, and techniques used in project
- Reflections about what was learned
- Self-evaluation of ideas and strategies

Homework Projects

- Clippings, images, articles glued onto the page
- Written comments
- Parent or student comments

Presentation

- Attractive front and back cover
- Writing is neat, readable, and carefully done
- Well organized
- Shows sparks of creativity

I prefer using a small blank book or artist's sketchbook that students keep with them all the time for drawing, working out ideas, and collecting sources of information that relate to art problems they're trying to solve. Students frequently make a series of thumbnail sketches to try out different approaches to ideas they want to express in larger projects. Somehow the blank, unlined pages encourage drawing, experimenting with new techniques, and additional practice. You can ask students to jot down thoughts about what they are trying to show and how they feel about their work.

SHOPTALK

Hubbard, Ruth Shagoury and Karen Ernst, eds. *New Entries: Learning by Writing and Drawing*. Portsmouth, New Hampshire: Heinemann, 1996.

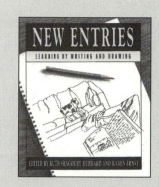

Shagoury and Ernst write, "Making images is as natural as speaking. In fact, it is a language—a way to communicate, think, express, and explore. When pictures and words work together to create meaning, literacy's potential expands." The thirteen educators who contributed to *New Entries* share ways they connect visual arts to language arts as well as to their own lives. Teachers from all levels—elementary school through college—invite you into their classrooms and show how writing, art, and reading can be combined in various subject areas. The stories of these teachers and their classroom experiences are a great place from which to start your own explorations.

When I ask students to write in their journals or sketchbooks, I provide a few questions to get them started and ask for help in brainstorming a list of additional questions about visual art or related topics. Students add questions to our class list whenever one occurs to them. We choose one question—the "Question of the Day"—from our list and students write and draw their responses. I've found that with this approach, students become more interested and curious about art in our everyday world, and their list of questions is endless. Here are some of their questions we've explored:

- Who is an artist?
- Who is art for?
- What makes an artist famous?
- What is beauty?
- Why do artists paint weird stuff?
- Why do we study dead artists?
- How many dollars is *The Irises* really worth?
- What makes modern art modern?
- Why are some paintings called art and others called junk?
- How would my sculpture of a big spoon get in a museum?
- Why do artists draw things that don't look real?
- Why is a bunch of metal called a great sculpture?

- Does the title matter?
- Why do people get excited about a line that doesn't look like anything?
- Why do people whisper at the museum?

Los Angeles artist-educator Laurine DiRocco encourages young learners to work like artists, using their sketchbooks as a place for visual meandering, collecting visual ideas, making rough sketches, and gathering data for future reference and elaboration. Students fill their sketchbooks with diagrams and drawings, making "picture notes" of what they see, hear, and think about throughout the day. The students draw their impressions of math activities, stories, and conversations, and frequently gather in small clusters to share their information. They compare pictures, describe details, and write down or dictate phrases and sentences so the class has a public record of what they believe is significant.

Field Notes: Teacher-To-Teacher

I've found that my preschoolers as well as older students enjoy the freedom of drawing in their sketchbooks. They really feel ownership over their drawings. Our sketchbook format is fairly unstructured so students can choose what they want to include. Sometimes the sketches become stories that we write together or act out. At other times, the sketches become full-blown easel paintings that we hang in our classroom for all to admire.

Laurine DiRocco
Artist-Educator
Los Angeles, California

Students' sketchbooks are visual process journals that promote reflection and help DiRocco and her students launch classroom discussions. Sometimes students talk about a scientific investigation they've recorded visually over time. For example, students were working on the theme of "change." In science, they were studying how vegetables grow, how they're used, and how long they last. Some students brought in pumpkins and wondered if carved pumpkins and uncarved pumpkins rot the same way. Another time they decided to see which would sprout faster on a moist paper towel, dry kidney beans, soaked kidney beans, or toasted pumpkin seeds. Each day of the experiment, students ran eagerly to get their sketchbooks to make drawings and take note of any changes they perceived. DiRocco keeps the sketchbooks out on a table and invites students to share them with her. One of the most respectful teachers I've ever worked with, she engages students in personal conferences—a series of conversations about the content of their sketchbooks—taking anecdotal notes which help her to guide students in their learning. In this way, she is able to give students individual attention while assessing their development and levels of confidence.

Audiotapes

Tom Still, a teacher friend in Agoura Hills, California, gave me the idea of using audiotapes to provide students with ongoing feedback about their writing—feedback they could also share with their parents. In my case, I used audiotapes as a way for students to assess their artwork. I asked each child to bring in a blank audiotape and explained that we would be having conversations about their art projects during the year. (If students can't afford the audiotape, see if your department or school can write it into their budget. Or, perhaps local stores or manufacturers will donate the tapes to your class.)

Let students know that you will be giving them feedback, posing questions, and asking them to discuss their thoughts about their work with you on a regular basis either on tape or in person. Tell them they can take the tape home, along with their artwork, to share with their families, or they can listen to it in class at the listening center. This is an effective strategy for keeping families informed about how we integrate visual arts into the curriculum. Parents and other family members often seek out ways to connect what their children are learning in class to activities going on in their community—museums, craft shows, local artisans. Another benefit I've seen is that students are willing to rework their projects, incorporate independent practice, or do more research after considering feedback from family members, teachers, peers, and their own self-reflections.

Parents and other family members often seek out ways to connect what their children are learning in class to activities going on in their community—museums, craft shows, local artisans.

Anecdotal Records

Another way to assess students as they work is to observe and make notes to capture "snapshots" of what students do and say, and jot down your interactions. This strategy helps me pay particular attention to specific students I'm trying to reach. If I want to increase a student's level of participation and engagement in learning, or find more successful ways of working with him or her, I gather data to use in developing a plan of action with the student.

Interviews and Inventories

Interviews and inventories are an effective way to find out what art experiences children have had. You might interview in groups or individually. Provide a written questionnaire or tape your interviews. Ask students about their art experiences as a way of getting to know their interests and expand their knowledge and understanding of art in the classroom and in their world. You may want to include open-ended questions or requests such as these:

- What art fair, museum, or art galleries have you visited?
- What is your favorite piece of art? Who made it?
- Do you know anyone who is an artist? What kind of artist?
- If you could do anything you wanted to in art, what would it be? Why?
- What will knowing about art help you do?
- What books have you read about art or artists?
- What movies, television programs, or computer games do you like? Why?
- Make or bring a piece of artwork from home that you'd like to share with your classmates and be ready to give a little history about it and tell why the piece is important or special to you.

Checklists

Create lists of skills, art elements, and mediums you want your students to practice, and then invite self-assessment and personal record-keeping. Faith Dennis, vice principal at Bathgate Elementary School in Mission Viejo, California, sets up an art table with tools, materials, resources, task cards, checklists, and guidelines for independent practice, cleanup, and record-keeping. Students take responsibility for their learning and assess themselves from start to finish. You can create a checklist for any tasks you'd like students to practice in addition to projects they can finish on their own.

Checklist for Working on Art Elements, Skills, and Mediums

Name_____

I am working on _____

Directions

1. Decide what art element, skill, or medium you wish to practice.
2. Get the appropriate materials and create your samples.
3. Date your samples on the back, let them dry, and put them in your portfolio.
4. Clean up as agreed.
5. Assess your progress. You might find the following icons useful in your self-evaluation.

o.k.   good start   fine   terrific

Date	Art Element	Skill	Technique	Sample	Progress
2/4	*Lines*	*Contrasting thick and thin lines*	*Marker*	*Chart*	
2/6	*Lines*	*Creating dark and light tones*	*Marker/pencil*	*Design*	

Field Notes: Teacher-To-Teacher

I found in my study of second-language sixth graders that students given the opportunity both to draw and to write during a test were able to express their understanding of world history content knowledge and raise their scores. I also found that this assessment strategy increased students' level of engagement. What I think this means for teachers is that we all have something to gain by examining the use of arts to promote equal access to achievement for all students, and especially limited-English speaking learners.

Karen DeJarnette
Director of Research
The Galef Institute

Photographs and Videotapes

Whenever possible, videotape or photograph students in the process of working, especially if they are working on three-dimensional pieces such as wood carvings, wire sculptures, or large pieces that are difficult to keep in a portfolio. Camera shots combined with written student reflections work well for documenting and creating a "history" of the learning event. Char Girard and Dick Jacobsen, sixth-grade teachers at Emma Shuey School in Rosemead, California, teach students how to use a camcorder to document their process as well as how to put together a finished videotape of a finished performance. Students look at the tapes to learn how to improve their presentations, and are highly motivated to share their expertise with their peers.

Self-Reflection

I've already mentioned journals, learning logs, and sketchbooks as places for thinking on paper. I believe that one of the tricks to self-reflection is modeling the process yourself so that students acquire the habit of writing down their thoughts about their processes as creative and imaginative learners and artists. You may want to demonstrate what you mean by self-reflection by "thinking out loud" while writing a personal reflection in your journal.

As you ask students to reflect on their work, think of questions that will guide them into the habit of making connections between how they work in art and what they do in other parts of their learning lives. Request that they think about expressive qualities and creative problem-solving strategies. You may want to pose questions such as:

- What were you trying to express in your work?
- In what ways were you successful?
- What did you notice about the way you worked?
- What would you do differently?
- What new questions do you have?
- So far, what's the most interesting discovery you've made about yourself as a creative problem-solver and learner?
- How will you use what you've learned in this project in other areas of learning in and outside of school?
- What do you want to try next?
- What do you want people to remember about your artwork?

Seeing and discussing art from different times, places, and cultures helps students include many perspectives in their own work.

Class Critiques

I find that holding class critiques has dual benefits. First, it gives students ways to participate in developing the ability to look at, respond to, analyze, appreciate, and discuss their artwork in a safe environment. Second, it gives me a chance to interact with students, hear them converse with each other and listen to what needs and interests they have so as to help me assess and adjust my teaching decisions.

Begin by asking students to look at a piece of work with the intent of learning from it. Ask students to pin up their artwork and gather around for a critique which will help them develop their own emerging skills as artists. Set the tone for students to make comments that are positive and focused on the goals of the project. Invite students to discuss special visual effects they are attempting to achieve—an expression of melancholy in a person's face, a mood of serenity and calm—and point them to particular skills and criteria that will help them be successful.

You may want to introduce students to the works of artists as sources of inspiration, or ask students to provide each other with helpful hints or techniques. Offering examples of art from many cultures and regions of the world opens students' eyes to the creative richness that is part of our world history. Seeing and discussing art from different times, places, and cultures helps students include many perspectives in their own work. Ultimately, it's important for students to realize that people can have different opinions and that there is no one right answer but many points of view.

A "Three-Two-One" strategy is an easy and safe way to begin holding class critiques because students focus on constructive criticism. Model the procedure to help students understand what is expected. Ask them to write down or talk about what they observe in a work of art. That's basic. Students can only offer comments on what they see in the artwork. The strategy can be used when holding critiques in whole group, small groups, pairs, and triads.

> Observe and comment on *three* things you really like about this artwork. Be sure to use the visual arts vocabulary.
>
> Tell the artist **two** ways you'd like to see a part or idea further developed.
>
> Tell the artist *one* unique characteristic of his or her style or talent you've noticed by seeing this work.

Wall Chart

You can create a simple wall chart by posting a large sheet of craft paper on a wall identifying the art problem to be solved, the goals of the project, and learning skills. Invite students to record observations of the progress they see their peers making as they work on the assigned project. For example, "I see Jenny choosing contrasting colors like red and green. I like the way Zack is mixing red, blue, and orange to come up with a murky brownish purple for the bottom of his mountain." Students help create a supportive, student-centered learning community by encouraging each other with feedback on skills, techniques, and work habits.

Discussions and Conversations about Art

Holding discussions and conversations about art encourages critical thinking and analysis. For me, there's a certain joy in engaging in talk about the impact and influence of art in our everyday lives. Our conversations connect us all to art experiences that people have shared across centuries in a variety of cultures, contexts, and historical settings. Conversations about art can be either informal or formal, depending on the goals you have in mind. Think of discussions as specific mini-lessons that help students discover the many ways art is relevant to their lives.

When you begin a conversation about art, have students look at images and ask open-ended questions. Encourage them to look deeply into the work with the intent of understanding and enjoying it and to use the vocabulary of visual arts to describe what they see. Help students understand they can talk about works of art without labeling them either as "good" or "bad," and

DIALOGUE

What categories of learning do I want to assess?

_____

_____

What guidance can I provide students so they are involved in ongoing assessment as their project evolves?

_____

_____

that they are developing insightful ways to think about what they see and how it applies to their own habits of working.

Jeffrey Dorsey, a visual artist with the Pittsburgh Center for the Arts, works with students and teachers in the Pittsburgh area. He frequently initiates conversations about art by bringing in his own paintings to show that artists are alive and well and part of the community. Dorsey starts a conversation by asking students to look at one of his paintings while posing questions such as, "What's going on here? Tell me what you see. Look some more. What else is going on?" His goal is to have students begin chatting with him about what he's creating and trying to say. He encourages students to make connections to anything in the present or past that may be significant to them as an idea or theme. What Dorsey wants students to understand is that artists are continuously interacting thoughtfully with ideas and making creative choices as they work. As student artists, they can follow a similar process.

You can use discussions and conversations that present possibilities for integrating visual art with music, dance, literature, language arts, or social studies by using who, what, when, where, how, and why questions. For example, you may decide to focus on the theme of celebration and its importance in marking special events in everyday life. You may also want to emphasize the concept of change, or similarities and differences. You could introduce a theme by showing students two paintings: Renoir's _Dancing at the Moulin de la Galette_ (1876), of a couple dancing outdoors, and Thomas Hart Benton's _City Activities with Dance Hall_ (1930), of dancing indoors. As students look at the similarities and differences, they'll discover the paintings were done at different times. They'll note who is in the paintings and what people were celebrating. Student speculation and questions lead them to research into social studies, literature, poetry, music, or other studies to discover ways people celebrate. To encourage inquiry you might ask questions such as:

- Who do you see?
- What is going on? How do you know?
- When does this take place? What time of day? What time in history? How will you find out?
- Where is this happening? What city or country?
- How do the people in the picture feel? How do you know?
- Why is this event important? Why do you think the artist chose to portray this particular event in this way?

When we ask open-ended questions and let students follow their own line of inquiry, we help them make discoveries and connections to art, to other areas of the curriculum, and to lifelong learning.

I use the following assessment categories to help my students and me keep track of our learning.

When we ask open-ended questions and let students follow their own line of inquiry, we help them make discoveries and connections to art, to other areas of the curriculum, and to lifelong learning.

Assessment Categories

Content

_____ accuracy of content knowledge in curriculum areas and understanding of the concepts and themes

Development

_____ evidence of research

_____ integration of concepts into a thoughtful whole

Presentation of Performance

_____ integration of skills and techniques

_____ craftsmanship

_____ organization

_____ expressive qualities

Collaboration

_____ individual contributions and responsibility

_____ group cooperation

_____ work habits

Self-assessment

_____ journals

_____ checklists

_____ group portfolio

Our assessment strategies continue to evolve and emerge as we find out what works best for us and for our students. Perhaps a systematic way to think about integrating art, assessment, and learning is to think about the overarching goals of your program: what you want your students to learn; how you want them to learn; and what you want to know about your students as learners and yourself as a professional educator. The artifacts, records, and evidence of the learning processes collected over time will show authentically and in multiple ways what you and your students are accomplishing.

Chapter 7
Art as a Daily Affair

Art ignites the imaginations of diverse learners and motivates them to stay engaged.

Even when I'm not in school, I think I am an artist because I see things that go right into my imagination, and artists use their imaginations every day.

Liliana, age 10

Art should be an everyday event. We want children to make visual arts an integral part of their lives—and thus be able to apply the skills and knowledge to other areas of their school and everyday experience. Consequently, we have to be on the lookout for learning experiences that bring the use and enjoyment of art into focus. For example, for some children it means being able to draw or paint what they see or feel; for others it might mean seeing the story in a painting and finding deep satisfaction in the expressiveness of the image. What I've seen as an educator and heard through teachers' accounts is that art ignites the imaginations of diverse learners and motivates them to stay engaged. Students who are developing talent in art apply and transfer their knowledge and skills across multiple subject areas.

In this chapter, I'll share my classroom stories and those of other teachers who infuse art across the curriculum. These snapshots of classroom practice help to create a picture of what's possible. Looking into classrooms also shows us that making art a daily affair calls for a process of change that challenges our assumptions about teaching and learning, about being professional educators. Indeed, the road to transforming habits is not easy, yet the results are immensely satisfying and enlightening.

Yuki Yoshino team-teaches a second- and third-grade combination class of deaf and hearing students in a regular classroom in Burbank, California. She reminds us that visceral learning experiences—that is physical experiences—and their integration into the life of the classroom are important for adults and children. Following is Yoshino's discovery about the arts and learning.

Using Art Every Day—Yuki Yoshino's Discovery

I knew all about gesture drawing and working from a model. My eyes and arm understood this very well. This was my college experience and my after-school pursuit. It was a visceral adult experience. I lived it; I worked at it. During the day, I team-taught reading, writing, math, social studies, science, health, and physical education to deaf and hearing students. This too was a visceral experience. I lived it; I worked at it. Sometimes I threw in an art lesson, but it was more often than not an opportunity for children to express themselves without clarity of purpose. I wasn't sure how to share purposeful art with my students. I kept my two lives separate.

That changed the summer I attended an Open Institute of The Mid-South California Arts Project. From that gathering of arts educators in drama, visual arts, dance, and music, I began to think about "big pictures" in curriculum, using what I knew as a classroom teacher to make connections to what the arts offered. I figured out a way to integrate art purposefully and was eager to take a risk to try things out. I could integrate the big picture of art into reading and math, and the big picture of reading and math into art. If I focused on the big ideas of each subject area, I could provide deep experiences that would help students clarify and understand the concepts they needed to know in all three subjects. Ideas could be mutually supported and I could still teach the content and skills of each subject area.

I began by asking my second- and third-grade students to take turns as models, moving, gesturing, and freezing in a pose while their classmates locked their eyes on the movements of the model. The students practiced drawing the poses by making lines in the air. Then they filled large sheets of paper with gesture drawings made with large, flat crayons. After ten- or twenty-second poses and several drawings, students analyzed their best work. They worked with concentration and intensity. I guided these visceral experiences for my students. I helped them make connections between movement patterns and math patterns by having them count as the models moved on the beat and held energetic poses.

When students shared their movement studies, they made connections between modeling, gesturing, drawing, and dancing. I asked them to describe their work in writing, and they demonstrated clear understanding. My students connected the analysis of shape and balance in movement and in

Students who are developing talent in art apply and transfer their knowledge and skills across multiple subject areas.

I think a healthy and exciting tension exists between purpose and playfulness—a tension that sets the stage for feeling adventurous about taking risks in a dynamic learning community.

drawing with similar concepts in math and science. We made connections to main ideas, such as strength, in literature and reading and how they translate to what you want to emphasize in drawing and dancing. I knew students were seeing how one idea leads to the next when they could begin to see that their understanding of math patterns, for example, became clearly communicated in art, and even more clearly to themselves. I really knew that things were different when ten-year-old Chris, a former student, came by my classroom and exclaimed, "This is like an art studio. Why didn't we do anything like this two years ago?"

Unpacking the learning. As Yoshino's reflection indicates, one idea leads to another and opportunities for learning abound if you open your mind to freeing up the curriculum with a combination of purpose and playfulness. Having a purpose in mind provides a basis for deciding what to teach as well as a context for guiding classroom experiences that have the potential to deepen learning. When I refer to a sense of playfulness, I mean that you take on imaginative approaches that allow you and your students to discover amazing connections that enrich the meaning of concepts and move beyond your expectations. I think a healthy and exciting tension exists between purpose and playfulness—a tension that sets the stage for feeling adventurous about taking risks in a dynamic learning community.

Making Art a Choice

In allowing for student choice, many teachers organize their classrooms by offering a variety of projects that provide opportunities for independent research and practice as well as for extending interests in the arts, reading, math, science, social studies, and other subjects. Offering students choice is a teaching and management strategy that allows us to step to the side and become classroom guides who encourage and nurture self-reliance in all learners.

Students share in the responsibility. I like students to take responsibility for directing their time by making a list of "jobs" they can choose to do on their own. This strategy allows for student choice and exploration of interests, and it also addresses the fact that students finish assignments at different times. More often than not, the jobs include learning through, with, or in art because students find the work enjoyable as well as challenging. I either organize several projects with the necessary materials, resources, and directions in lightweight, portable boxes that students work on at their table, or I set up work centers in the room with "help yourself" task cards. Frequently, students extend discoveries they've made about other subjects and design research projects or special tasks with and for their classmates. They take responsibility for gathering the resources, making task cards, sharing their expertise, and managing the work center. This way, every student is given a chance to be a teacher.

Offering students choice is a teaching and management strategy that allows us to step to the side and become classroom guides who encourage and nurture self-reliance in all learners.

One way to remind students of their independent learning opportunities is to create a chart listing the choices and posting it in a prominent spot in the classroom. Consider some of the choices I offer students and add to the list.

Make a Choice

Help yourself to a choice of learning opportunities. You may want to

- work at the art center
- finish integrated projects at your desk
- read a biography about an artist and create a poster
- write or draw in your journal or sketchbook
- use the computer for researching artists, authors, or architects
- write twenty questions about an artist of your choice
- make a crossword puzzle about your project
- create a "pictionary" of directions for a science project
- work on the classroom gallery
- make a project that connects art with _____ (you decide)
- design an art project that integrates three big ideas in _____ (you decide)
- find a famous quote about art; copy, decorate, and share it

- write a letter of praise to a student artist
- plan an arts awareness campaign
- plan an art quiz show
- invent a project of your own.

Students might also choose to create a "task card." The first of those below, written by students, prepared classmates for playing a quiz game.

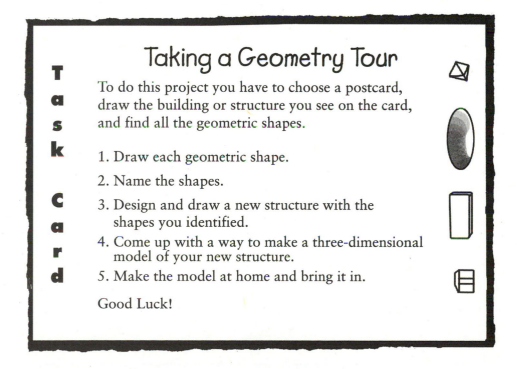

T a s k   c a r d

Frida Kahlo

All about Frida Kahlo:

To do this project you have to read, draw your answers, and make a decorated fact card with a caption to add to the stack.

1. Read about Frida Kahlo.
2. What are three important things about Frida Kahlo's life?
3. What do you like best about Frida Kahlo's work?
4. Make a creative Frida Kahlo fact card to share.
5. Clean up.

T a s k   c a r d

Taking a Geometry Tour

To do this project you have to choose a postcard, draw the building or structure you see on the card, and find all the geometric shapes.

1. Draw each geometric shape.
2. Name the shapes.
3. Design and draw a new structure with the shapes you identified.
4. Come up with a way to make a three-dimensional model of your new structure.
5. Make the model at home and bring it in.

Good Luck!

And, of course, part of independent learning is keeping track of what you're doing and reflecting on the process. A simple "Keeping Track" form has worked well for me and my students. Take a look at how Ginessa kept track of her work.

Keeping Track

Directions: Make sure you write the date, name of the choice you made, what you liked, and next steps you plan to take. Put the form in your journal for your weekly conference.

Name: Ginessa

Date	Choices	I liked	Next steps
4/3	Frida K Center	Seeing her portraits and colors	I want to read more about her
4/4	Frida	she was different I like her poses	I will look for more of her work
4/6	Frida	I found 2 facts	Go to the library

An Interdisciplinary Adventure—Carol Wright's Story

Carol Wright of Lawndale, California, engages her kindergartners in hands-on research, while teaching about the concept of "care." Using the *Different Ways of Knowing* curriculum module, *Families: Caring for One Another* as a guide, she focuses on several learning events grouped around the topic of food, and makes connections to literature, math, science, language arts, and literacy skills.

Wright planned a sequence of learning, including taking a field trip to a market and then having children paint still lifes of food. She envisioned introducing her students to two or three still-life paintings of food, and thought of the art experiences, vocabulary development, and use of imagery she could provide. She listed potential areas of learning and skills to remind herself of teachable moments and possible connections. Her list included

- basic needs
- jobs
- marketing
- estimation
- patterning
- graphing
- sorting
- geography
- directionality
- interviewing
- questioning
- cooperation
- collaboration
- following directions
- perseverance
- problem solving
- problem finding
- analyzing
- applying
- nutrition
- growing
- cooking
- observing
- recording
- interpreting information
- sharing information
- reporting
- reading
- writing
- painting
- drawing
- synthesizing
- recalling
- comprehending
- decision-making
- evaluating
- independence
- mathematics

Armed with drawing pads and pencils to sketch and record their observations and conversations, a camera to document the trip, and a list of questions for the market workers, Wright and her young researchers set off. Once at the market, the students inspected all the departments, browsing in every aisle. They stopped in the produce department to interview the produce manager with questions such as, "Where do you get the food? How do you decide how to arrange the foods?" and "What do you do with the old food?" The children inspected the orderly arrangement of fruits and vegetables, noting the vast assortment of squash and lettuce. They made sketches of the food and estimated the cost of buying enough produce for their entire kindergarten class. Then the children weighed, bagged, and bought sacks of apples, bananas, oranges, grapes, squash, celery, and potatoes with money provided by the Parent Teacher Association.

Back at school, Wright gathered students around her to record their market experience. Eager hands went up to help Wright chart the important events the children remembered. "We bought apples and talked to the man," volunteered Asanka. "The oranges cost too much money," said David, and Mendy offered, "The food looks like a rainbow." At the end of the debriefing session, the kindergarten researchers triumphantly read their chart together, sharing the success of their first level of research.

The next day, Wright displayed still-life paintings, such as Paul Cézanne's *Apples and Oranges*, Wayne Thiebaud's *Pie Counter*, and unusual works (all made up of produce) such as Giuseppe Arcimboldo's *Summer*. She invited students to compare and contrast the paintings, and charted their observations and comments. Two of the most frequently asked questions were, "How can every picture look so different?" and "Why do artists make the foods look so different?" As children compared the fruits and vegetables in the paintings to those they had purchased, they were amazed to find that they could actually see elements of art such as line, shape, color, and texture in some of the produce they had bought themselves. "Use your art detective eyes," Wright urged, as she encouraged students to look for similarities and differences in the paintings and to notice art elements. To help them see line designs, patterns, and textures, Wright and the children cut open some fruit and vegetables to observe. They also dipped samples of the food into tempera paint to explore printmaking. So that children could continue their research up close, Wright gave them postcards of still lifes to examine. She also set up a center with colored clay for making replicas of the fruits and vegetables they liked. This activity gave the children time to experiment with more hands-on learning while Wright observed them and took anecdotal notes to assess their levels of involvement, interest, and understanding.

Art Elements We See in Fruits and Vegetables			
Line	**Shape**	**Color**	**Texture**
Celery— straight	Oranges—round	Oranges—orange	Celery—smooth
Lettuce—wavy	Onions—round	Onions—yellow, white, purple	Broccoli—flowery
	Apples—round	Apples—red, yellow, green	Lettuce—leafy
	Lemons—oval	Lemons—yellow	

To help her students get started with painting, Wright gave them time to practice quick sketching techniques, to get their ideas down on paper. She also demonstrated how to use watercolors. Then she encouraged students to explore using watercolors, tempera, or oil pastels to find their comfort level and gain proficiency. At last the children were ready to begin painting. They worked in small groups and arranged the produce they had purchased into four still-life set-ups. Soon they were hard at work as artists, painting with authority and confidence. "I hung their masterpieces in our classroom gallery and the children were ecstatic," says Wright.

It didn't end there. Next, Wright and her kinders wrote a recipe for "Yummy Fruit Salad," made it together, and had a good laugh about eating their still lifes. They also wrote thank-you letters to the market workers. "What

Yummy Fruit Salad

- Wash the fruit
- Cut it into bite-size pieces
- Count four pieces of each kind of fruit and put them in a cup
- Add a pinch of coconut
- Add three mini-marshmallows
- Add one spoon of orange juice
- Mix
- Enjoy!

fascinated me," Wright explains, "was the cycle of learning—it just kept getting bigger and bigger. A parent volunteered to help us plant a vegetable garden outside our classroom. Children became expert guides when their families made trips to the market, and their enthusiasm and skill for creating illustrated books and reading the charts and recipes they had written together continued. They kept adding to their own learning."

Field Notes: Teacher-To-Teacher

I think of the impact that visual arts has had on all of my children, but Huong stands out. She remained silent in my class for several weeks, as I struggled to reach her. She worried me because she refused to talk or interact with the other children. Giving her a variety of art experiences—sketching, working with clay, painting with tempera and watercolors, allowing her time and space to work with the materials as she needed—seemed to draw her out. The other children began to notice and comment on Huong's art, and their encouragement gave her the confidence to speak up and share her ideas with all of us. That experience taught me an unforgettable lesson: children often know what words alone can't measure.

Carol Wright
Roosevelt Elementary School
Lawndale, California

Field Notes: Teacher-To-Teacher

To celebrate students' reading a particular piece of literature, I invite them to create any kind of artwork that either depicts specific comprehension of the literature or entices others to want to read the literature. Examples of student work include

- a circular mural divided into pie pieces showing various settings of the story
- paper squares with watercolor paintings that highlight important happenings and are sequenced into a quilt
- puppets created to represent character portrayals with an accompanying visual background theater.

Robin Potchka
Anderson Elementary School
Lawndale, California

Social Studies, Reading, and Art—Carol Umlas' Story

An excerpt from Carla Umlas' journal follows. It recounts how she included art to empower her first and second graders at Monlux School in Van Nuys, California, to read and to love reading.

In February I wanted to help the children celebrate the achievements of famous African Americans, so I turned to *America's Family Stories*, the *Different Ways of Knowing* curriculum module, to help me get started. The first book I read aloud was Deborah Hopkinson's *Sweet Clara and the Freedom Quilt*—about a young girl's dreams of following the Underground Railroad to freedom. This fit in perfectly because I had taken the students on a field trip to the Gene Autry Heritage Museum to see a quilt exhibition, so they had experiences to build upon. In the story, Clara sews a quilt that maps out the secret route to Canada. The children were fascinated with the story and the wonderful paintings by James Ransome. We read the story several times and they came to understand that quilts could tell good stories just like books. Because the children took such an interest in geography and astronomy—which are brought up in Clara's story—we took a side trip to learn more about those subjects. Next I introduced Jeanette Winter's picture book, *Follow the Drinking Gourd*—about one family's journey from slavery to freedom along the Underground Railroad—which led to a rich discussion. Finally, I read Faith Ringgold's *Dinner at Aunt Connie's House*, and that did it. My students simply identified with Melody and Lonnie and the paintings of famous African Americans in the attic.

Langston Hughes

Deana

"I am Langston Hughes. I was born in Missouri in 1902. I was a writer of poems, books, plays and songs. I created theater groups in Harlem, Los Angeles and Chicago."

Oron

WILLIAM CHRISTOPHER (W.C.) HANDY

"I am William Christopher (W.C.) Handy. i was born in 1873 in Florence, Alabama. I was a musician. I am known as the "Father of the Blues.""

Pia

Mary Jane Mcleod Bethune

"My dream was education. My name is Mary McLead Bethune. I was born in 1875 in South Carolina. I founded a college and i also founded the National Council of Negro Women."

Jesse Owens

"I am Jesse Owens. I was born in Alabama in 1913. I won three gold medals in the 1936 World Olympics in Germany."

Alexander

They were completely taken with this story of portraits that talk, or tell a story, and asked me to read it to them time and again. During free time, the children flocked to look at the book and read it over and over to themselves.

The children and I talked about making a talking quilt like Aunt Connie's, so I put together a variety of resources for their use, and invited them to learn about other famous African Americans. We agreed that every student could choose their own person, complete the research, and share what they had learned with others. In that way, each child could become an expert. The students pored over illustrations of the men and women and, using their observational skills, came up with preliminary sketches and final drawings. Students were so proud of their research and their art when they had their portraits "talk" about their accomplishments. Their understanding of fractions and geometry almost occurred as an afterthought, because we were so intent on making history and art come together in our quilt.

Unpacking the learning. Reflecting on the project, Umlas concludes, "The best part for me about the talking portraits and reading the stories, particularly *Dinner at Aunt Connie's House*, is that every student wanted to read more and I had to put lots of other books around the room. I knew they were on their way. They were going to know how to read—and love it."

Nothing makes teachers happier than to have students achieve goals that they value—Umlas is no exception. She was thrilled to see the progress of one student in particular, first grader Matthew. Says Umlas, "In September, Matthew could barely read the sentence, 'Come out Chip' from the first grade preprimer, *New Friends*. By January, Matthew was so interested that, when

everyone had gone on to the cafeteria for lunch, he sat there reading about Jackie Robinson. He read that book every day for weeks at DEAR (Drop Everything and Read) time. With an enormous smile on his face, he came to tell me each day something else he had learned about Jackie Robinson. When June rolled around, it gave me so much pleasure to give Matthew that book."

"I am Jackie Robinson. I was born in Georgia in 1918. I was the first African American player on a major league team. I played baseball for the Brooklyn Dodgers. i was also the first African American to be inducted into the Baseball Hall of Fame."

Including Art in Everything We Do—Julie Flanagan's Story

In Julie Flanagan's fourth-grade class at Anderson Elementary School in Lawndale, California, students comfortably use sketching as a method to generate ideas. Students feel free to move to an art center to practice drawing skills. They include drawing or painting as part of voluntary homework assignments they do with their families when they assume the role of teacher at home. Flanagan allows students to decide how they want to integrate the use of drawing, painting, modeling with clay, or computer-generated art. Flanagan says, "I can't even remember when we didn't have some form of art in my classroom. I think my students just expect to put art into everything. It can be at the beginning to get ideas, when they are stuck, to help them work out a sequence, or as a final expression. There's writing, math, social studies, science, and everything else we have to do; and there's always art, music, and some drama connected to the learning. If I don't ask students to include some form of art, they do it on their own. If they need to research an artist, a picture, or an approach in art, they use our classroom computer as a resource, and they appreciate and remember their research. My students come up with the ideas and invent their own strategies for making art meaningful to them and their learning."

Unpacking the learning. Flanagan's students have become so comfortable with drawing that they visit the technology center at school and use computer programs such as Kidpix, Kidworks Deluxe, and HyperStudio to create illustrated picture books, diagrams, and graphics with ease. Students manipulate the tools of technology with confidence, and transfer strategies for solving problems and expressing themselves across the curriculum to such an extent that Flanagan says she is awestruck with their ability to design and resolve creative problems on computers. Flanagan asks students to work in pairs to research the desert from the *Different Ways of Knowing* curriculum module, *A Geography Journey: Adventuring in the United States*. Students gather information from a variety of resources and investigate desert environments, animals, habitats, and issues of protection and survival. Flanagan

Students manipulate the tools of technology with confidence, and transfer strategies for solving problems and expressing themselves across the curriculum

asks them to become "experts" on desert life by creating a series of illustrated mini-books. They also write brochures and reports that they dramatize
to show what they have learned. In this kind of project, Flanagan is able to
integrate district language arts standards with social studies and the visual
and performing arts thus providing multiple ways for all her students to participate successfully. Throughout the process, Flanagan observes the
student's eagerness to participate in all phases of the project. She takes special
note of the high expectations they have for themselves as they complete each
part of the assignment. Flanagan says she finds it gratifying that her students
have positive attitudes about their ability to learn. "They are constantly challenging themselves, and can do more than I expect."

Art Specialists and Classroom Teachers Working Together

Val Dellas, an experienced art specialist in the Penn Hills School District of
Pennsylvania, had every reason to believe she was doing a great job. The
principal and teachers all gave her good ratings and loved what she did with
their students. Parents also reacted positively to her work. Without any dif-
ficulty, in forty-five minutes, Dellas says she could direct students in an orderly
art lesson, demonstrate and teach an art concept, and be assured that 90 to 95
percent of the projects her students produced would be successful. After
students created good work and cleaned up, they marched back to their classrooms in straight lines. The teachers then had art projects to put up on their
bulletin boards. According to Dellas, "Everyone was happy. But sure enough,
I always thought something was missing. There had to be more to this than
teaching a kid how to cut a valentine on a fold or make a design using
positive and negative space."

When Dellas began to work with teachers implementing *Different Ways of Knowing*, she began to develop a new perspective. She writes, "More recently, I've been involved in professional development and firsthand experiences with teachers and students who are using art as an integral part of an integrated, interdisciplinary curriculum. I am seeing that art is no longer a frill, but a means of understanding. I am seeing students learn and think, and my own classroom has become a sort of learning lab where students can demonstrate and connect their learning. These days, my art lessons begin with kids entering my room and discussing what they know about a subject area they're studying. I devise an art problem for them to solve, making connections to the knowledge they've acquired in their other studies. I still demonstrate media and techniques they can use to solve their art problem, and am mindful of teaching art concepts and completing my responsibilities to the art curriculum."

Dellas has also rethought her presentation of the art curriculum. She now makes available in her room a variety of resources for student research, such as history and literature books, art prints, and audiotapes. Students work alone or in small groups, and the room buzzes with conversation about art. Dellas admits that the art projects take longer because, as she puts it, "this is no longer just art that you put on a bulletin board." She says, "I continually ask students to take their thinking a little further, and that takes time. It's worth it because their art is so much richer. These are art expressions of what students have learned in all of the disciplines. In fact, a fifth grader commented that he's noticed that everything his teacher talks about, I talk about, and everything that I talk about, his teacher talks about. He said to me, 'I'll tell you one thing, art is a lot harder, but I like it a lot. I'm having fun.' I thought to myself, it sure is harder. I'm asking him to think and respond, make connections, and take responsibility for his learning. In fact, I'm having more fun teaching than I've had in years. It wasn't fun in the beginning. It was change and I resisted, but with coaching, support, and the encouragement of colleagues, my paradigm shifted. I started seeing all of the possibilities instead of all the roadblocks. It was exciting!'

Third-grade classroom teacher Jane Vernon and visual arts specialist Cindy May of Hickory Grove Elementary in Bloomfield Hills, Michigan, also work hand in hand. They believe their professional partnership sends a powerful message to their students. They model collaboration, helping students see that skills and content knowledge are not isolated in separate compartments or classrooms. For example

- Vernon teaches students fractions in her classroom, and May connects to their learning her art lessons on color theory.

I am seeing students learn and think, and my own classroom has become a sort of learning lab where students can demonstrate and connect their learning.

- Students observe that Vernon and May use the same math terminology.
- Students apply the color theory they learn with May to illustrations in a book they're reading in Vernon's class.

Let's expand on the last example. In social studies class, Vernon introduced students to the topic of immigration by reading aloud *The First Thanksgiving* by Jean Craighead George. To acquaint them with the importance of vivid imagery, she worked with May to guide students in analyzing the Thomas Locker oil paintings that illustrated the Pilgrim's journey to the New World. The teachers asked students to see ways the illustrations enhanced the narrative and facilitated the discussion. May asked students to create watercolor paintings to interpret their understanding of the themes of exploration and discovery she and Vernon had presented in social studies, language arts, and art. In their watercolors, the students applied their knowledge of horizon, object placement, imagery, and color theory. Both teachers found that the stories students wrote to accompany their paintings contained rich details and beautiful descriptive writing. In the role of an arts and culture reporter, May interviewed the children about their watercolors, and found they had a deep understanding of the historical perspectives surrounding the events they portrayed in their paintings as well as sophisticated knowledge of the art concepts they applied. Vernon and May look upon their children's expressions of learning as an interdisciplinary integration that they value and support because of the connections they are able to make beyond the classroom door. They are resources to each other as well as to their students.

The stories students wrote to accompany their paintings contained rich details and beautiful descriptive writing.

S H O P T A L K

George, Jean Craighead. *The First Thanksgiving*. Illustrated by Thomas Locker. New York: Philomel Books, 1993.

Jean Craighead George gives us a sensitive portrayal of the Pilgrims coming to the New World and the people, events, and environment they encounter as they shaped new lives for themselves. Artist Thomas Locker illuminates and enhances the mood, tone, and emotion of the story with subtle, glowing paintings that draw the reader into the moment and time. Using the art elements of color, shape, line, and texture as his vocabulary, Locker captures the realism of George's words.

Science, Geography, Literature, Technology, and Art

Mark Rodriguez is a math, science, and technology resource teacher at Roosevelt Elementary in Lawndale, California. During a Roosevelt summer school program integrating the *Different Ways of Knowing* module *A Geography Journey* across all grade levels, Rodriguez worked with middle school students to create multimedia projects using HyperStudio. *The Mountain That Loved a Bird*, written by Alice McLerran and illustrated by Eric Carle, was their point of departure. Rodriguez explains, "I chose this book because it incorporates concepts of science and geography—mountain formation, the ecosystem, effects of weather on plant and animal life, and biology—in a fictional context with beautiful artwork. At the same time students were learning science and geography concepts, they were developing skills in writing, storytelling, drawing, word processing, technology, and working collaboratively."

Rodriguez spent about five class periods introducing his students to HyperStudio software. They learned how to use the drawing tools, word processing features, sound, and transitions, as well as ways to move from one card to the next. Then he and his students read the story together and discussed it. Later, students regrouped in threes or fours to retell the story to each other. Then they did choral readings with gestures. After a brainstorming session to decide how they could integrate what they had learned from the book with HyperStudio, students decided to retell the story in their own words and create new illustrations. They prepared rough sketches of their graphic ideas on paper before moving to HyperStudio.

At the same time students were learning science and geography concepts, they were developing skills in writing, storytelling, drawing, word processing, technology, and working collaboratively.

In the spirit of Carle's illustrations in *The Mountain That Loved a Bird*, the students incorporated geometric shapes into the graphics. Some groups created abstract mountains, while others went for a more realistic look. Some groups created a script of dialogue; every group included some degree of sound. Rodriguez attributes the variety of student work to the "nontraditional" style of Carle's illustrations. "I wanted students to focus on the visual retelling of the story, so they added the text after they completed their artwork." Recognizing the value of public presentations, Rodriguez invited his students to share their work in a culminating districtwide geography museum. Each group had their turn to present. They sat in front of the computer and answered questions while Rodriguez projected their work on the big screen.

Reflecting on the project, Rodriguez says, "Kids had so many different opportunities to shine—visual, spatial, linguistic, artistic. This entire project made me a firm believer in the theory of multiple intelligences."

Math and Art Connections

As you plan your math lessons, think about how students can apply their understanding of concepts, such as patterns, to art. When children make quilts, create tile patterns and tessellations, and use manipulatives such as pattern blocks, they are seeing relationships, applying their understanding of the concept of pattern, and developing their spatial sense.

Tessellations. *Different Ways of Knowing* instructional coach Freda Klotter of Lexington, Kentucky, invites students to create tessellations, a learning experience that helps them understand that a repeated geometric figure becomes a pattern. She shows them examples of tessellating patterns in floor tiling, brick driveways, certain mosaic designs, and Islamic art. Then they learn how to create their own tessellations with a "nibble and slide" technique. First, they make a simple template beginning with a 3" x 3" square. They cut a nibble and matching notch from opposite sides of the square.

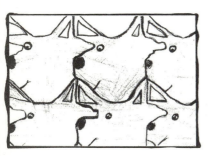

A tessellation made by students in Louise Nielsen's fifth grade class in Rio Rancho, New Mexico.

Next, they trace and slide the template again and again across the page until they've covered the sheet of paper. Students can learn to use their templates for estimating and measuring area and perimeter on graph paper. They can put together a group tessellation—a chance to practice their co-operative learning and problem-solving skills. When Klotter shared the student's work with the art teacher at their school, the art teacher used the opportunity to take their interest in tessellations to teach warm and cool colors and the element of contrast. "It's amazing to me that as the children explored the elements of art, they came to understand a math concept which in turn made them more aware of patterns in the whole environment," says Klotter. "Creating their own tessellations took a lot of perseverance, which did not go unnoticed by their families who applauded their efforts. And their resulting pieces evolved into beautiful works of art."

Mobiles. A hanging mobile is an undertaking that combines the mathematical skill of balance with the challenge of thinking spatially and aesthetically. It is an art form that students can use to display their understanding of concepts and themes across the curriculum. The mobile offers natural opportunities for creative problem solving. If you think of the theme of "balance"—in government, in our ecosystem, in health, and in our lives—it lends itself to connections across the curriculum. A mobile then works well as an expressive art form for communicating both physically and metaphorically student's understanding of the concept.

As the children explored the elements of art, they came to understand a math concept which in turn made them more aware of patterns in the whole environment.

The components for making a mobile include

- suspended shapes
- thin wood, plastic, or metal tubing
- wire, thread, or nylon cord.

SHOPTALK

Bawden, Juliet. *Mobile Magic: Innovative Ideas for Airborne Accessories*. New York: Lorenz Books, 1996.

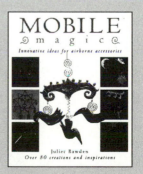

Here's a book that will give you and students countless ideas about what materials to use and how to make interesting, meaningful, and beautiful mobiles. Over forty projects, shown through a sequence of step-by-step photographs and instructions, will help start you on your way.

I begin simply by giving students two thin sticks or tubing to form a crossbar, several yards of nylon cord, and sheets of assorted heavy-gauge tagboard. Then I have children think about what they want to express in their mobile and invite them to design shapes that illustrate the visual and physical concepts of balance. I tell students that the mobile must function as an integrated work that can be hung from a ceiling. It will be seen from all sides and be artistically expressive. In addition to working with balance, students have to consider solving technical and aesthetic problems. I ask them to consider questions such as:

- What do I want my mobile to express?
- How will the mobile look and function as an integrated structure?
- What length should each piece of nylon cord be?
- What shapes will I create that look well together?
- How will the size and number of the shapes affect the overall balance of the mobile?
- What elements of art and principles of design should I use?
- How will the shapes be attached to the nylon cord?

My students have also enjoyed the challenge of using a circular shape, such as a wooden or metal ring or embroidery hoop, at the top of their mobile. When I ask students to create mobiles, I make sure that I show them works by Alexander Calder who created both hanging and standing mobiles. Calder's *The Mobile* (1959), hangs in the International Arrivals Building of the John F. Kennedy airport in New York, and his *Four Elements* (1962) in Stockholm. Exposing students to works such as these helps to develop their appreciation of the form and provides new sources of art for them to study and learn from.

Maskmaking. Maskmaking incorporates the mathematical concept of symmetry, and also provides opportunities to delve into the history and appreciation of the art form as a performance tool and means of expression. Moreover, masks offer curriculum links to theater, music, dance, media arts, folklore, and literature as well to as cultural studies that are part of the social studies. Through the use of masks, students can portray historical characters, speak lines, and deliver a convincing and expressive point of view with more effectiveness than they might without the use of masks. I like to introduce maskmaking by asking students to visualize the "faces" they wear every day and to consider the possibility that every person wears and changes masks when their mood and emotions change.

Children can make masks with all sorts of materials, including

- papier maché
- paper plates
- paper bags
- cardboard or tagboard
- drawings on clear acetate
- decorated clay

Maskmaking incorporates the mathematical concept of symmetry, and also provides opportunities to delve into the history and appreciation of the art form as a performance tool and means of expression.

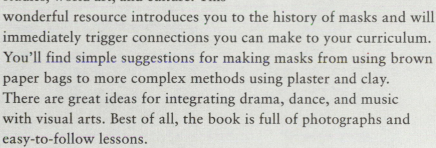

S H O P T A L K

Sivin, Carole. *Maskmaking*. Worcester, Massachusetts: Davis Publications, 1986.

If you're going to make masks, you've got to have this book.

Students enjoy maskmaking and make connections to literature, history, social studies, world art, and culture. This wonderful resource introduces you to the history of masks and will immediately trigger connections you can make to your curriculum. You'll find simple suggestions for making masks from using brown paper bags to more complex methods using plaster and clay. There are great ideas for integrating drama, dance, and music with visual arts. Best of all, the book is full of photographs and easy-to-follow lessons.

In each of these examples, I'm sure you can picture the different ways students can make productive and creative connections between mathematics and art. Such connections lead children to understand ways that math assists them in their artistic expressions.

Masks offer curriculum links to theater, music, dance, media arts, folklore, and literature as well as to cultural studies that are part of social studies.

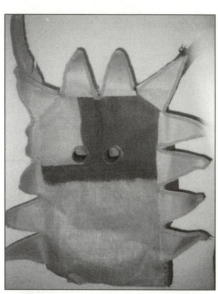

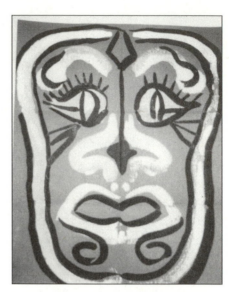

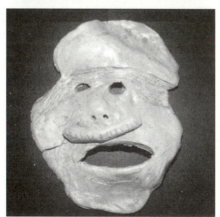

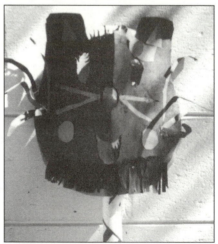

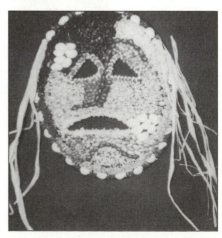

Integrating Art Through Group Projects

Teachers frequently engage students in group projects as a culminating activity. I believe that projects such as murals, tabletop displays, puppet dramatizations, and presentations give students opportunities to learn about the give and take of creative problem solving. Students have opportunities to practice making critical decisions about their responsibilities to a group effort, learn to present their points of view, and resolve conflicts that may have to do as much with creating art as with how to work in a group. In today's world, the ability to cooperate and collaborate is a vital skill that we can begin teaching early on. While students are preparing their group projects, you will want to offer mini-lessons that help them understand and apply the specific content and skills they will need to be successful in demonstrating knowledge of the art form and subjects they are integrating.

Murals. To help students value and appreciate the mural as a form of expression, I've facilitated mini-lessons on the history of murals, on painters who expressed themselves as muralists, and on the impact of murals as public art. These mini-lessons are designed to lead students on investigations of murals from a variety of perspectives

In today's world, the ability to cooperate and collaborate is a vital skill that we can begin teaching early on.

- exploring the work of muralists from ancient to contemporary times and the mural as a unique form of expression
- researching the social, political, and economic contexts in which murals have been created
- applying skills related to scale, proportion, and measurement
- exploring environmental and ecological issues surrounding the maintenance and preservation of murals and other public works of art.

Yuki Yoshino's student, Alyssa, sees the value of making a mural. Besides the synthesis of content learning, which Yoshino assesses, Alyssa describes how the work makes her feel, "The big paper...it makes me feel free."

Jan Cohn, who has taught kindergarten through sixth grade, worked with me at Seeds University Elementary School, the laboratory school at UCLA, where we developed and implemented interdisciplinary group learning projects for teams of sixty to eighty children. We developed units on gardening, health, and manufacturing and organized them around the universal theme of "systems." The systems theme helped us organize and integrate concepts and topics across the curriculum. We wanted to help students

- develop the skills to function successfully in a variety of roles so they could work cooperatively in different types of groups
- understand the concept of interdependence and realize that, to a great extent, people are responsible to each other in a well-functioning democratic system.

Mural-Making Evaluation Sheet

Group name _____ Date _____

Group members	How we each did
1. _____	_____
2. _____	_____
3. _____	_____
4. _____	_____
5. _____	_____

We are responsible for _____

Jobs

1. drawing _____

2. coloring _____

3. cutting _____

4. pasting _____

5. cleaning up _____

We think our group worked well ___ yes ___ no ___ so-so

We did our best because _____

We need to improve on _____

The best worker today was _____

We need help with _____

We liked what we did ___ yes ___ no ___ so-so

We did well on job number ___ 1 ___ 2 ___ 3 ___ 4 ___ 5

We could do better on job number ___ 1 ___ 2 ___ 3 ___ 4 ___ 5

We all worked together ___ yes ___ no ___ so-so

Tomorrow, we will _____

_____

_____

_____

Cohn and I conducted informal surveys to determine student interests within the systems theme. In this way, students could identify and use some of their own ideas in their group mural. We included mural-making as one of our major hands-on learning projects because it involves group decision-making, individual accountability, problem solving, and critical and creative thinking. These were all areas in which we wanted to help students develop comfort and skills. We were both committed to having students learn through experience, and we viewed discussion and self-evaluation as integral to the process of responsive teaching and learning. Cohn and I learned to guide the process by observing our students' interactions and the daily progress they made in small-group, individual, and large-group settings. We saw that long-term projects gave us opportunities to recognize different learning styles and strengths in our students.

For a project such as a group mural, Cohn and I generally engaged our five-to eight-year-old learners in the process of setting individual and group standards. They worked with us to establish criteria for the final product as well as for evaluating works-in-progress. We designed simple tools for the students to use to plan their work and assess themselves. With students, we developed checkpoints along the way which enabled them to evaluate themselves and helped us know where we needed to provide additional guidance or move ahead. Cohn and I opened and closed the day with class meetings and a discussion of the day's activities. This schedule gave us a chance to hear from the children and share our reflections of group membership. We asked students to mediate conflicts by bringing issues out in a reasonable manner so that these could be discussed and resolved by group members.

We were always mindful of the "invisible" learnings we wanted students to value: the power of individuals working together and contributing to the achievement of a worthy goal.

Reflecting on our goals for group projects, Cohn and I used multiple lenses for identifying the purpose of a project. On one level, we took into account the skills and content we expected students to learn. They had to understand, synthesize, and communicate concepts at more than superficial levels. On another level, Cohn and I were always mindful of the "invisible" learnings we wanted students to value: the power of individuals working together and contributing to the achievement of a worthy goal.

Social Studies, Literature, Writing, and Art

Art integrated with social studies, literature, and writing can deepen students' understanding of social studies content, literary concepts, and writing and art techniques. For example, I asked my fifth and sixth graders to write, illustrate, and publish an epic poem as we studied

- the epic poem as a genre in literature
- ancient Greek civilization
- illustration and color mixing.

DIALOGUE

Ask yourself these questions as you develop standards and criteria for group work with your students:

What do my students have to know and do in order to demonstrate understanding of each content area (for example, social studies and art) integrated in the group project?

_____

_____

What do children already know? What do they have to learn? How will their learning be facilitated?

_____

_____

What group interaction and decision-making skills will students need in order to be successful?

_____

_____

What are acceptable standards for demonstrating understanding or the acquisition of skills in each of the content areas? What is exemplary? What is unacceptable?

_____

_____

What elements of creative and artistic expression should be evident in the final product?

_____

_____

What information must the artwork convey about agreed-upon learning?

_____

_____

During this twelve-week social studies unit, we immersed ourselves in the daily life and culture of the ancient Greeks and in related topics under the umbrella of heroism. One of my goals in our literature study was to enable students to understand the hero cycle and structure of the epic in order to assume the roles of authors and illustrators in creating their own stories. I reorganized the class day into a series of half-day workshops to give us long blocks of sustained learning in different subjects areas related to the theme. Students used afternoons for individual and paired study periods. I offered small group and whole class mini-lessons linking ideas and content that supported the generalizations students were beginning to make about the qualities of heroism, heroes, and heroines. Within this ambitious cycle of learning, students exhibited their knowledge of the hero in literature: they integrated concepts of Greek art and culture by writing, illustrating, and publishing an epic poem. Every student produced a handmade book—an opportunity to create a highly personal first edition as well as appreciate the book as an art form.

Betty, one of my sixth graders, began drafting her epic. She used painting and drawing in a creative cycle to clarify and enrich both visual and literary expressions. She pored over her sketches of Greek life, looked at artifacts, and reread Greek myths in preparation for crafting her narrative. She developed visual metaphors for Chloe, the heroine in her myth, and tested the accuracy and expressiveness of her words against her visual representations,

S H O P T A L K

Olson, Janet L. *Envisioning Writing: Toward an Integration of Drawing and Writing*. Portsmouth, New Hampshire: Heinemann, 1992.

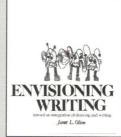

Olson suggests that drawing can help students write. Drawing belongs in the writing process, she proposes, since the unique interaction among drawing, thinking, and writing supports visual and verbal learning and benefits all types of learners. Olson has found that students use drawing as a tool to clarify or elaborate thoughts, to work out settings and plots, to translate images and thoughts into pictures on paper, and then from pictures into writing. Olson offers teachers methods and strategies for becoming informed about what students are able to express through drawing. This book challenges us to acknowledge what we don't know but need to find out if we want to help all students to communicate effectively.

holding to the exacting standards she had set for herself. For example, in her poem, she described Chloe's "azure-blue eyes." After examining her painting, she decided she had to correct the color-mixing formula she had made to intensify the color of Chloe's eyes. Betty described Chloe's cheeks as "red" in one of her written drafts and revised it to read "blushing rose" after smelling, touching, and blending colors to reproduce the subtle shading of the Double Delight roses we were painting.

I was thrilled. Betty was making connections between her art and writing, moving between verbal and visual images with ease. It was not unusual to see Betty poring over a passage of her epic with a paintbrush or pencil in her hand—poised to draw—so that she could work out the descriptive quality of her writing. Although I knew that Betty was enthusiastic and talented in art, I was surprised to see her willingness to make multiple drafts and write until she had reached a level of quality she pictured for herself. At the conclusion of the project, I asked students to reflect upon themselves as authors, by responding in their journals. Betty expressed her thoughts eloquently about her own process in becoming an author:

> I can't believe that I wrote and illustrated this story myself. I published this whole epic myself. It is good. I like my ideas. I always wanted to be an artist because I like art better than writing. But maybe I could write stories and illustrate them. I like to write and write and write.

SHOPTALK

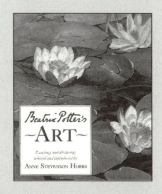

Hobbs, Anne Stevenson, ed. *Beatrix Potter's Art*. New York: The Penguin Group, 1989.

Beatrix Potter is celebrated for her books for children. However, the tremendous success of her writing has, in some ways, overshadowed her work as an artist. As Hobbs shows, "Many of her most original pieces, independently invented and untouched by publishers, were neither exhibited nor printed in her lifetime. Her essentially private and unshowy art demands and deserves close attention." Potter's work is elegant in both its simplicity and sophistication. Hobbs' book is a wonderful way to broaden students' knowledge and exposure to an artist with whom they may be familiar.

Getting to know artists and their art. Just as students take pride in creating works of art and using various art forms to express themselves, they also enjoy the process of becoming knowledgeable about art as a subject of study. They like becoming experts who are able to hold good conversations with each other about the life and work of different artists and periods of art. When art becomes part of the classroom curriculum, students see artists as real people and as contributors to the culture of a time and period.

One strategy I've used to promote this exposure is to include artists—along with scientists, musicians, politicians, historians, and other public figures—when I introduce students to the genre of biography. Students' exposure to artists informs them about art forms, techniques, and the periods in which the artists lived. Students naturally dig for more information. Khaim, a talented eleven-year-old cartoonist with a sardonic sense of humor, chose to

create a four-panel comic strip to demonstrate his knowledge of Van Gogh's life to share with younger readers. Khaim felt that young children would be more interested in a comic strip than a long book or report. As Khaim told me, "This is like an ad to get little people to pay attention to Van Gogh before you read them the whole story." With a survey that he had conducted during recess and lunchtime breaks, Khaim argued his point so well that I agreed to alter my written assignment. The class was ecstatic, and Khaim became a very special hero.

On another occasion, my nine-, ten-, and eleven-year-old students expressed an interest in Paul Cézanne. They wanted to become well informed about his life as an artist, his artistic decisions, and his techniques. Students read biographies, articles, and short essays about Cézanne. They analyzed and made comparisons of several of his paintings, adapted and interpreted his methods in their own paintings, and wrote critiques of his work. In the process, they assumed the roles of artist, historian, and critic. I planned a month-long unit with part of the time devoted to small group and individual research. Other time blocks were spent on class work, independent study time, and homework. In the role of art critic, students studied reproductions and biographical notes I had organized into a series of art packs of Cézanne's work. They analyzed the works, discussed them in small groups, and took part in dramatic simulations with students playing the roles of the artist and the critics defending their points of view. As a follow-up activity, I asked children to write letters to Cézanne to share their opinions of his work. The ensuing letters gave me an opportunity to assess students' writing skills and their understanding of the art elements and principles of design.

Dear Paul,

The one painting of yours that I don't like is "Still Life with Basket of Apples!" The reason I don't like this painting is because nothing is happening unlike "Mont Sainte Victoire." In this painting everything is alive: The trees, plants, and the mountain itself. In your still life of apples nothing is alive. The background is just gray, the wine bottle has no interest to me with its blue and green color. The apples look stale with bits of yellow-brown. The only interesting thing is how the yellow bread is stacked. The mood is boring, while things happen in the "Mont."

As this letter comes to an end, I'd like you to know, Paul, that you created more good paintings than bad.

Adam

Dear Mr. Cézanne,

I am writing to you because I wanted to discuss two of your paintings. The first one is "Still Life with Cupid." I feel this painting is very expressive because of the expression of love and sadness on Cupid's face.

The painting has asymmetrical balance because of the way cupid is leaning. I see balance throughout the painting and rhythm in the apples, oranges, and squash painted below cupid. I think Cupid catches your eye the most, although he is ivory white. That color blends in very well with the faded reds, oranges, and yellows. I think you thought about details and color in this painting and that's why I enjoyed studying it.

The second painting I would like to discuss is "Mount St. Victoire." This painting gives me an eerie feeling because of the dull blues, greens, yellows, and purples. This painting looks asymmetrical (just like "Still Life with Cupid") because the huge triangle shape that is the mountain leans a certain way. There are many shrubs in the valley below the mountain that are in the reported shape of triangles. Looking at them makes me feel like I'm in a maze.

When I compare these two paintings, it seems like your colors and technique changed dramatically. But some things haven't changed: the balance throughout both paintings and rhythm haven't changed. There is rhythm in the shrubs in the valley below the mountain in Mount St. Victoire, and rhythm in the fruits and vegetables below Cupid in "Still Life with Cupid."

Meghann.

As you integrate art studies into your school day, facilitating the exploration of strategies and tools, keep in mind that all children can learn to express themselves with clarity and authenticity, and take personal satisfaction in their work. Some of your strategies will be modest, some more complex; but all should be focused on the learners and on every possible way to nurture and empower them.

Working with a Community of Artists

Virtually every community has residents who engage in art either as professionals or in their spare time. Conduct a search among friends and parents to uncover folks who have artistic talents or art expertise who will enjoy participating in art activities with students and teachers. Los Angeles visual arts educator, Hawley Hussey, works with classroom teachers, schools, and organizations to provide hands-on workshops that engage adults and children as working partners. Specializing in murals and projects that bring children and community artists together, Hussey introduces students to universal themes such as respect, interdependence, and care. Making art and learning accessible for all students, she integrates creative writing and poetry with art, building visual metaphors and images that carry into descriptive writing.

Not long ago, the Galef Institute in Los Angeles, commissioned Hussey to create, in collaboration with students, a series of murals and paintings for its offices—works that would represent the Institute's commitment to students and the arts. Working with sixty students whose ages ranged between eight and ten, and with six local teachers, Hussey and fellow artist Cecil Schmidt organized the youngsters into six teams of art apprentices. Hussey was the "art director" and Schmidt was the "mural captain." Hussey and

Schmidt talked through ideas and drew up preliminary plans which were based on social studies themes in the Institute's *Different Ways of Knowing* curriculum modules. The students knew from the start that as they worked on their parts of the murals at school, another team of adult artists would be working in their studios to create huge backdrops. Ultimately their work would be integrated and displayed at the Galef Institute. This proved to be a very exhilarating and motivating idea.

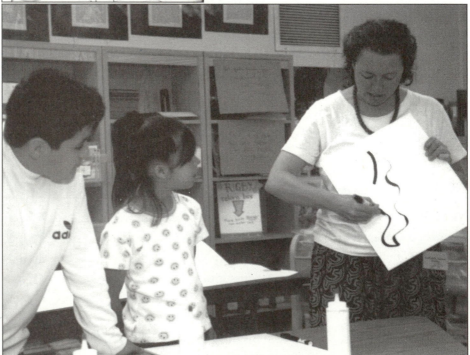

For three days, the media room of Anderson Elementary in Lawndale, California, became a thriving art studio. Like set designers creating their special part of the scene, students worked on discrete pieces of the murals. Teachers worked alongside their students and took notes of techniques and feedback Hussey used to encourage students to get the results she was seeking. Later, these teachers applied their experiences in facilitating follow-up lessons in their classrooms.

The murals were assembled and installed at the Galef Institute by the adult artists. At a reception that honored the student artists and participating teachers, Hussey congratulated them on their first "installation." The students enjoyed finding their own work that was part of the whole. They also took pleasure in seeing themselves at work in large photographs displayed throughout the Galef offices. The students spoke of how much they enjoyed creating their artwork and how it expanded their knowledge of art and artists in the community.

A Public Classroom Gallery

A powerful addition to the regular display of artwork is a public gallery in your classroom dedicated to showing something special, such as the process of creating a mural or a variety of approaches to an art technique or a theme. The benefits are far-reaching. All at once, you can acknowledge student artists, introduce them to the public, gather public support for your art program, and expose viewers to different approaches to creative problem solving. To honor all students as artists, I make it a practice to display the work of every

student during the school year. You can hang works-in-progress as well as final products to inform the audience about the various stages of work.

A public gallery or display area requires some planning, along with an uncluttered wall space in your classroom or school hallway set aside for this purpose. You can present the gallery as a design project: ask students to work in small groups to create a plan that they'll present to a panel of "experts" for final approval. Students can help organize the space, gather materials, and mount and hang the images. All this activity helps students develop an awareness of both design and public space aesthetics. In addition, students are prompted to think about the role of art in the community. Designing gallery space for artwork also offers opportunities to engage students in research on museums, galleries, and careers in the visual arts. Along the same lines, a teaching gallery presents an opportunity to invite museum educators and docents to your classroom. These experts can present community education programs, and become resources to you and your students.

Starting the classroom gallery. Visiting and becoming familiar with museums and galleries helps students design their classroom gallery. I invite parents to take their children to museums and galleries to see interesting works of art and to see how different exhibits are installed. I ask students to make diagrams of installations so that they are aware of wall space, groupings of work, architectural features of a gallery space, and the aesthetic presentation of artwork. I want them to be aware of frames and mats as part of the overall presentation of work and how these help create an exciting art

Field Notes: Teacher-To-Teacher

I maintain a prominent place in my sixth-grade classroom right by the door labeled "The Louvre Museum of Room 12." This is where students display their art in attractive frames next to the work of a well-known artist. Sometimes we paint like a master artist, and I put the artist's work up with my students' art next to it. Space is limited, but I hang several pieces of art there for a week. Eventually all my students have a spot in the "Louvre Museum."

Terry Karsh
Anderson Elementary School
Lawndale, California

experience for the viewer. From their research, students get ideas about how to set up an exhibit, offer suggestions, and even search out materials to create frames and mats. You can invite parents to contribute their time and energy to this kind of project as well. Here are a few hints to get you started with ideas for framing student work and starting a student gallery

- Reuse empty gift boxes for shadow frames.
- Cover stiff cardboard with fabric or wallpaper to use for matting.
- Choose a color mat or frame that complements the picture.
- Hang pictures in a unified way.
- Label pictures with the name of the artist and title of the work.
- Put clay figures or sculptures on painted shoeboxes, wooden blocks, or bricks to showcase them.
- Collect old frames and repaint them.
- Mount all artwork—without staples—on nice construction paper.
- Treat artwork with respect.

You and students can extend invitations to parents and local business partners to sponsor and support your teaching gallery. They can be helpful in providing materials, resources, and contacts for public display space in your community. Students can write letters or create invitations to welcome parents and friends to see their work. They can hold an opening reception with light refreshments to kick off the gallery opening, serving as docents.

Dear Parents and Friends,

You'll be so pleased to know that the work of _____ is currently on exhibit in our gallery. We have been studying the theme of "celebrations" for the past few weeks. We invite you to see our exhibit, titled "Rites and Rituals." This is a collection of masks that we have created from found objects and recycled materials. Please come join us. The gallery hours are flexible Monday through Friday.

Regards,

The Artists of Room 9

Here's an example of an information card for Brian's piece of art.

Title: Movement to the Max

Artist: Brian J., age 10

The Art Problem: To create the illusion of movement and action.

The Process: To warm up and loosen our drawing arms, we moved in space in twos, and practiced gesture drawings on classified sections of the newspaper, since the paper was cheap. We exaggerated our movements, stopped action, and made more drawings, this time on white paper. Next we "deconstructed" the drawings to cut out the geometric shapes and made overlapping figures tumbling in space. I made a lot of studies and chose the one I liked best.

Materials and techniques: We used mixed media—crayons, watercolor wash, and markers on crumpled brown paper.

Artist's reflections: I like my final work. I thought moving my body wouldn't help at first, but it did. "Movement to the Max" is the title I came up with because I felt maxed. The big figure—that's me, moving.

DIALOGUE

As I gather information to put on placards for the art gallery, what facts do I want to share with viewers?

_____

_____

What will help the audience learn about the creative problem, learning process, the methods we used, and what the artists think about their work?

_____

_____

Will I include

_____ the art problem students were asked to solve?

_____ the learning process?

_____ the materials and methods used?

_____ the name and age of student artists?

_____ students' personal reflections?

How can students help to compose their own placards?

_____

_____

Art in Our Community

I still remember poring over slides and reproductions of well-known art images when I was a teenager, trying to imagine the real power of Picasso's *Guernica*. Reading about the work and studying details was rewarding, but I always felt that I needed to see the work for myself. Years later, when I did come face to face with Picasso's monumental work, I was overcome with the effect it had on me. I was standing before a work that was familiar, yet brand new. I experienced the intensity and compelling nature of *Guernica* on a very moving and personal level. Both the image and the experience remain with me to this day.

"Guernica" by Pablo Picasso. Museo Nacional Centro de Arte Reina Sofia. Archivo fotografico Museo Nacional Centro de Arte Reina Sofia. (C) 2000 Estate of Pablo Picasso/Artists Rights Society (ARS), New York.

My experience with *Guernica* has contributed to my belief that children need similar opportunities to visit museums, galleries, and public places where art is viewed. Children's impression of their field trips will vary greatly, but all of it is vital. The experience helps them gain impressions of art in public and private institutions. Students can then develop an awareness of their relationship to the formal settings in which art is housed. Children may notice the architecture, the interior of different galleries, the landscaping, the frames on the works, the variety of artworks and forms, or simply the elegance or grandeur of a space. All of these experiences are of a visual nature, and they build children's awareness of art and their attitudes toward cultural institutions.

Because they have seen reproductions and slides of particular paintings and art forms, or grappled with similar ideas and themes in their own art, students may come to recognize certain works as old friends. I'm reminded of nine-year-old Marcus, a student I met in Compton, California, who remarked, "I'm going to see my Van Gogh." When I asked Marcus what he meant, he replied, "His yellow bed is mine, and I have to see how yellow." Apparently Marcus had a personal need to find out more so that he could compare his own bedroom painting to that of Van Gogh's. These acts of seeing and responding to art, finding out more, and knowing where and how people show art are important for a number of reasons. One important reason is that the museum tours and field trips connect students to a community of artists past and present who bridge cultures, time, and place. Students, in turn, are given access to new information and perhaps new perceptions of the value of art in their lives.

Relationships with Artists and Art Organizations

I've come to think of a community of professional artists as people who contribute to the wealth of the arts we see. These professionals include artisans, craftspeople, painters, sculptors, designers, architects, photographers, video and media artists, animators, and creative designers, among others. Your students and your school can develop relationships with professional people and organizations who can extend and enrich your students' learning and creativity as well as establish cultural ties that will enhance your entire school community. In that regard, you might

- contact the arts council in your state for a listing of arts organizations and cultural and art events
- contact local museums for special tours and art education programs that can be brought to your school site and offered at the museum as outreach programs for children and families
- contact the fine art, arts and humanities, design, and media arts departments at your local college or university to see if they'll become partners to support your students' interests
- call local art galleries and dealers to arrange for tours and speakers
- write a letter home to parents and families asking them to share their knowledge and expertise in visual art
- put your name on gallery and museum mailing lists to receive catalogs and calendars of events

Museum tours and field trips connect students to a community of artists past and present who bridge cultures, time, and place.

"Bedroom at Arles" by Vincent Van Gogh, Dutch, 1852-1980, oil on canvas, 1888, 73.6 x 92.3 sm, Helen Birch Bartlett Memorial Collection, 1926.417 photograph ©1998, The Art Institute of Chicago. All right reserved.

- make a habit of checking your community newspaper for news of special exhibitions, continuing shows, and cultural affairs
- contact local companies that specialize in film and video production, advertising, and public relations to let them know of your interest in artist volunteers
- check your local television guide and public television station for notification of special broadcasts about the visual and performing arts.

In addition to your local community, you'll find a wealth of online services and magazines to provide you with additional connections.

- The Smithsonian Institution at http://www.si.edu/educate.html offers teaching resources including inquiry-based lesson plans tied to primary sources and museum collections.
- WebMuseum at http://sunsite.unc.edu/wm/ takes you to the virtual Louvre in Paris.
- ArtsEdtalk at http://www.artsednet.getty.edu/ArtsEdNet/Resources/Chalmers/index.html encourages viewers to look for common themes, such as pluralism, in art.

Visiting artists. Students enjoy occasions when they can learn from painters, photographers, designers, and other people who have careers in different fields of art. On one memorable occasion, I invited my friend Frank Page, a Los Angeles graphic designer and illustrator, to share his work with my class of fifth graders. Page brought a large portfolio of works-in-progress as well as finished illustrations and printed material. To the student's amazement, he showed pages and pages of thumbnail sketches that resulted in two versions of a final illustration that, ultimately, his client did not purchase. He led them in an effective analysis of his work that developed their sense of aesthetics, a sense which they had once thought belonged only to discussions about paintings. My students were intrigued with the technical aspects of putting together mass-produced artwork. They also showed an interest in Page's creative process, quizzing him about the decisions that led him to become a designer who functioned successfully in the worlds of art and business. Indeed, Page helped the students make new connections about the role of artists and designers, and careers they could choose. Once again, another door of learning was opened.

Another time, I asked visual artist Harriet Germain—a vibrant and energetic septuagenarian—to share her experiences with my class. Germain worked with handmade papers to create somewhat sculptural forms, rich with natural fibers and textures. Because she could offer tremendous insights about living the life of a creative person and parent, I thought she would be an inspiration to my students. Germain brought examples of

her work and demonstrated the intricacies, patience, and artistic skills of papermaking, charming students into wanting to make their own paper. We worked out a plan to integrate the project with a unit on recycling: lint gathered from our dryers at home along with interesting scraps and "stuff" found in walks around school became the raw materials for our papermaking project. Germain was our coach and partner throughout the process. The results were more than rewarding for the unique opportunity it gave students to interact with an individual who was part artist, part teacher, and part philosopher.

Before you invite an artist to your classroom or go on a field trip to an artist's studio, find out what questions and issues students want to discuss. Encourage them to brainstorm what they want to know; then generate a set of questions and have them practice. Ask students to explain why they want to know these things. Here are some questions that students frequently ask professional artists.

- Where do you get your ideas?
- How did you get started in art?
- What made you choose your career as an artist?
- How much money do you usually make?

- What do you like about your work?
- What's the hardest problem you ever had to solve?

After the visit, be sure to have your students write thank-you letters. Consider including accompanying student art with their notes.

Putting It All Together

As educators, we often ask ourselves what tools and strategies we can use to help us make a difference with our students. How can we tap into every child's natural inclination to create, to make things, and to use art as a language of expression? How do we empower every student to put it all together?

I believe it begins with each of us reaching inward, taking risks, and going beyond what we already know. I think it's about having a mind open to experiences and opportunities. Not long ago I facilitated a visual arts workshop in Los Angeles, and invited teachers to reflect upon their day's experiences in making, looking, and thinking about the art they had created. I asked them to write about how their experience affected them personally and to think about new attitudes or insights they might have as a result of their participation. After a period of quiet, sustained writing, Jutti Marsh, a 5th grade teacher at Loreto School, shared her thoughts with the group. I provide Marsh's reflection as an invitation to ponder our experiences and what they may mean for us and for our students.

Art Has No Mistakes—Just Opportunities

There,
That wasn't so terrible.
Hey!
It's okay!
I can do it!
A community of artists.

Life.
A blank sheet of paper.
I'm afraid.
What if I make a mistake?
I try.
A stroke
On the blank canvas of life.
There,
Not bad.
Actually, it's good.
Others are on this journey.
A community of artists.

A room full of art supplies.
Paper, brushes, paint, water.
Some non-traditional art materials.
A room full of potential.
A blank sheet of paper
Dares you to mark it,
Stain it.
There,
It's done.
You can't erase paint!
Commitment.
Share with others—
Not so painful.
A community of artists.

A room full of children
Afraid of art.
"Mine isn't good enough."
"Teacher won't like it."
"My friend will laugh."
Blank paper challenge.
Make a mark!
A community of artists.

Like Jutti, I believe we start by taking personal responsibility for infusing art as a way of knowing into our lives every day. We create for ourselves and our students opportunities that invite engagement in art as a subject of study and as a strategy for integrating life's learning experiences. Some of those experiences occur right in the classroom; others happen beyond the classroom walls. Through our own demonstrations of risk-taking, joyful participation, and reflection, we model the connections between art and the wonder of being a learner. Our students walk alongside us as partners in the adventure of putting it all together.

Professional Bibliography

Anderson, Richard L. *Calliope's Sister: A Comparative Study of Philosophies of Art.* Englewood Cliffs, New Jersey: Prentice Hall, 1990.

Aker, Suzanne. *What Comes in 2's, 3's, & 4's?* Illustrated by Bernie Karlin. New York: Simon & Schuster, 1990.

Architecture and Construction. Voyages of Discovery Series. New York: Scholastic, 1994.

Arnheim, Rudolf. *Visual Thinking.* Berkeley, California: University of California Press, 1969.

Art Education. National Art Education Association. Reston, Virginia.

———. National Art Education Association, vol. 49, no. 5 (1996)

———. National Art Education Association, vol. 50, no. 4 (1997)

The Art of Sculpture. Voyages of Discovery Series. New York: Scholastic, 1994.

Arts and Activities. Publishers' Development Corporation. San Diego, California. A monthly journal.

Ashton, Dore, ed. *Picasso on Art: A Selection of Views.* New York: Da Capo Press, Inc., 1988.

Baumgardner, Jeannette Mahan. *60 Art Projects for Children: Painting, Clay, Puppets, Prints, Masks, and More.* New York: Clarkson Potter, 1993.

Bawden, Juliet. *Mobile Magic: Innovative Ideas for Airborne Accessories.* New York: Lorenz Books, 1996.

Beattie, Donna Kay. *Assessment in Art Education*. Art Education in Practice Series. Worcester, Massachusetts: Davis Publications, 1997.

Beckwith, Barbara et al. "Symposium: Arts As Education" part 2, *Harvard Educational Review*, vol. 61, no. 3 (1991).

Bird, Lois. *Assessment: Continuous Learning*. Strategies for Teaching and Learning Professional Library series, The Galef Institute. York, Maine: Stenhouse Publishers, 1995.

Brown, Maurice and Diana Korzenik. *Art Making and Education*. Champaign: University of Illinois Press, 1993.

Burns, Marilyn. *Math for Smarty Pants*. Illustrated by Martha Weston. Boston: Little, Brown & Company, 1982.

Cecil, Nancy Lee and Phyllis Lauritzen. *Literacy and the Arts for the Integrated Classroom: Alternative Ways of Knowing*. White Plains, New York: Longman, 1994.

Chapman, Laura H. *Approaches to Art in Education*. New York: Harcourt, Brace Janovich, 1978.

Clark, Hiro, ed. *Picasso: In His Words*. San Francisco: Collins Publishers, 1993.

Cohen, Elaine Pear and Ruth Straus Gainer. *Art: Another Language for Learning*. Portsmouth, New Hampshire: Heinemann, 1995.

Consortium of National Arts Education Associations. *National Standards for Arts Education: Dance, Music, Theatre, Visual Arts: What Every Young American Should Know and Be Able to Do in the Arts*. Reston, Virginia: Music Educators National Conference, 1994.

Crews, Donald. *Ten Black Dots*. New York: Greenwillow Books, 1986.

DeJarnette, Karen. "The Arts and Knowing: An Experimental Study of the Potential of the Visual Arts for Assessing Academic Learning." PhD diss., University of California, Los Angeles, 1996.

Dee, Ruby. *Two Ways to Count to Ten*. Illustrated by Susan Meddaugh. New York: Henry Holt, 1988.

Different Ways of Knowing. A Geography Journey: Adventuring in the United States. Los Angeles, California: Galef Institute, 1996.

———. *America's Family Stories*. Los Angeles, California: Galef Institute, 1996.

———. *Families: Caring for One Another*. Los Angeles, California: Galef Institute, 1996.

Dorros, Arthur. *Tonight Is Carnaval*. New York: Dutton, 1991.

Dunn, Charles. *Conversations in Paint: A Notebook of Fundamentals*. New York: Workman Publishing Company, 1995.

Duchting, Hajo. *Wassily Kandinsky*. Koln, Germany: Benedikt Taschen, 1991.

Edwards, Betty. *Drawing on the Artist Within*. New York: Simon and Schuster, 1986.

————. *Drawing on the Right Side of the Brain: A Course in Enhancing Creativity and Artistic Confidence*. Los Angeles: J. P. Tarcher, 1979.

Edwards, Carolyn, Lella Gandini and George Forman, eds. *The Hundred Languages of Children: The Reggio Emilia Approach to Early Childhood Education*. Norwood, New Jersey: Ablex Publishing Company, 1993.

Eisner, Elliot W. *Cognition and Curriculum: A Basis for Deciding What To Teach*. New York: Longman, 1982.

Epstein, Vivian Sheldon. *History of Women Artists for Children*. Denver, Colorado: VSE Publisher, 1987.

Ernst, Karen. *Picturing Learning*. Portsmouth, New Hampshire: Heinemann, 1994.

Escher, M.C. *M.C. Escher: The Graphic Work*. Koln, Germany: Benedikt Taschen, 1990.

Gardner, Howard. *Art, Mind and Brain: A Cognitive Approach to Creativity*. New York: Basic Books, Inc., 1982.

————. *Frames of Mind: The Theory of Multiple Intelligences*. New York: Basic Books, 1983.

————. *The Arts and Human Development*. New York: Basic Books, Inc., 1994.

————. *To Open Minds*. New York: Basic Books, Inc., 1989.

Gilot, Francoise and Carlton Lake. *Life with Picasso*. New York: Anchor Books/Doubleday, 1989.

Hart, Kate. *I Can Paint!* Portsmouth, New Hampshire: Heinemann, 1991.

Hinchman, Hannah. *A Life in Hand*. Salt Lake City, Utah: Peregrine Smith, Books, 1991.

The History of Printmaking. Voyages of Discovery Series. New York: Scholastic, 1994.

Hobbs, Anne Stevenson, ed. *Beatrix Potter's Art*. New York: The Penguin Group, 1989.

Hubbard, Ruth Shagoury and Karen Ernst, eds. *New Entries: Learning by Writing and Drawing*. Portsmouth, New Hampshire: Heinemann, 1996.

In the Process: A Visual Arts Portfolio Assessment Pilot Project. Carmichael: California Art Education Association, 1991.

Innovative Assessment: Portfolio Resources Bibliography. Portland, Oregon: Northwest Regional Educational Laboratory, 1993.

Jackson, Paul and Vivien Frank. *Origami and Papercraft: A Step-By-Step Guide*. New York: Crescent Books, 1988.

Johnson, Paul. *A Book of One's Own*. Illustrated by Jane Restall. Portsmouth, New Hampshire: Heinemann, 1992.

Johnson, Mia. *Teach Your Child To Draw: Bringing Out Your Child's Talents and Appreciation for Art*. Los Angeles: RGA Publishing, 1990.

Jonas, Ann. *Color Dance*. New York: Greenwillow Books, 1989.

Lanier, Vincent. *The Arts We See*. New York: Teachers College Press, 1982.

Locker, Thomas. *The Young Artist*. New York: Dial Books, 1989.

London, Peter. *No More Secondhand Art: Awakening the Artist Within*. Boston: Shambhala, 1989.

———. *Step Outside*. Portsmouth, New Hampshire: Heinemann, 1994.

Lopez, Barry. *Crow and Weasel*. Illustrations by Tom Pohrt. San Francisco, California: North Point Press, 1990.

MacDonald, Suse and Bill Oakes. *Numblers*. New York: Dial Books, 1988.

Mahy, Margaret. *The Seven Chinese Brothers*. Illustrated by Jean and Mou-sien Tseng. New York: Scholastic, 1990.

Mason, Antony. *Famous Artists: Matisse*. Hauppauge, New York: Barron's Educational Series, 1995.

Mittler, Gene. *Art in Focus*. Westerville, Ohio: Glencoe, 1994

McKim, Robert H. *Experiences in Visual Thinking*. Monterey, California: Brooks/Cole Publishing Co., 1980.

Munthe, Nelly. *Meet Matisse*. Boston: Little, Brown & Company, 1983.

National Standards for Visual and Performing Arts Education. Coordinated by Music Educators National Conference in collaboration with the American Alliance for Theatre and Education, the National Art Education Association, and the National Dance Association. Reston, Virginia: Music Educators National Conference (MENC), 1994.

K-12 Curriculum Frameworks in the Visual and Performing Arts. Lincoln, Nebraska: Nebraska Department of Education, 1996.

Ninety9: NAEA Preparing for the Millennium. Standards for Art Teacher Preparation. Reston, Virginia: National Art Education Association, 1999.

Olson, Janet L. *Envisioning Writing: Toward an Integration of Drawing and Writing*. Portsmouth, New Hampshire: Heinemann, 1992.

Paint and Painting. Voyages of Discovery Series. New York: Scholastic, 1994.

Partsch, Susanna. *Paul Klee, 1879-1940*. Koln, Germany: Benedikt Taschen, 1990.

Peppin, Anthea. *Nature in Art*. Millbrook Arts Library series. Brookfield, Connecticut: The Millbrook Press, 1992.

———. *People in Art*. Millbrook Arts Library series. Brookfield, Connecticut: The Millbrook Press, 1992.

————. *Places in Art*. Millbrook Arts Library series. Brookfield, Connecticut: The Millbrook Press, 1992.

Perkins, David N. *The Intelligent Eye: Learning To Think by Looking at Art*. Santa Monica, California: The Getty Center for Education in the Arts, 1994.

Prelude to Performance Assessment in the Arts, Kindergarten Through Grade Twelve. Sacramento: California Department of Education, 1993.

Raboff, Ernest. *Art for Children* series. New York: Harper & Row, 1988.

Remer, Jane. *Changing Schools through the Arts: How To Build on the Power of an Idea*. New York: ACA Books, 1990.

Richardson, Wendy and Jack. *The World of Art* series. Chicago, Illinois: Childrens Press, 1991.

Roalf, Peggy. *Looking at Paintings* series. New York: Hyperion Books, 1992.

Rowe, Gaelene. *Guiding Young Artists: Curriculum Ideas for Teachers*. Portsmouth, New Hampshire: Heinemann, 1989.

Roy, Susan and Jeremy Steele, eds. *Young Imagination: Writing and Artwork by Children of New South Wales*. Portsmouth, New Hampshire: Heinemann, 1989.

Schaefer, John. *Sight Unseen: The Art of Active Seeing*. Glenview, Illinois: GoodYear Books, 1995.

Schools, Communities, and the Arts: A Research Compendium. Developed on behalf of the National Endowment for the Arts. Tempe: Arizona State University. Morrison Institute for Public Policy, 1995.

Schuman, Jo Miles. *Art from Many Hands: Multicultural Art Projects*. Englewood Cliffs, New Jersey: Prentice-Hall, 1981.

Schwartz, David M. *If You Made a Million*. Illustrated by Steven Kellogg. New York: Lothrop, Lee and Shepard, 1989.

Short, Kathy G. *Literature as a Way of Knowing*. Strategies for Teaching and Learning Professional Library series, The Galef Institute. York, Maine: Stenhouse Publishers, 1997.

Sills, Leslie. *Inspirations: Stories About Women Artists*. Niles, Illinois: Albert Whitman, 1989.

Sivin, Carole. *Maskmaking*. Worcester, Massachusetts: Davis Publications, 1986.

Smithsonian Institution. *Smithsonian Postcard Books* series. Washington, D.C.: Smithsonian Institution Press, 1989.

Steward, Jan and Corita Kent. *Learning By Heart*. New York: Bantam Books, 1992.

Sturgis, Alexander. *Optical Illusions in Art*. New York: Sterling Publishing, 1996.

Szekely, George. *From Play to Art*. Portsmouth, New Hampshire: Heinemann, 1991.

Tejada, Irene. *Brown Bag Ideas from Many Cultures*. Worcester, Massachusetts: Davis Publications, Inc., 1993.

Topal, Cathy Weisman. *Children and Painting*. Worcester, Massachusetts: Davis Publications, 1992.

Turner, Robyn Montana. *Portraits of Women Artists for Children* series. Boston: Little, Brown & Company, 1991.

Venezia, Mike. *Getting To Know the World's Greatest Artists* series. Chicago, Illinois: Children's Press, 1988.

The Visual and Performing Arts Framework for California Public Schools: Kindergarten Through Grade Twelve. Sacramento, California: California Department of Education, 1996.

What the Painter Sees. Voyages of Discovery Series. New York: Scholastic, 1994.

Wilks, Mike. *The Ultimate Alphabet*. New York: Henry Holt and Company, 1986.

Williams, Helen. *Stories in Art*. Millbrook Arts Library series. Brookfield, Connecticut: The Millbrook Press, 1992.

Wilson, Brent. *Teaching Drawing from Art*. Worcester, Massachusetts: Davis Publications, 1987.

Wolf, Dennie Palmer and Nancy Pistone. *Taking Full Measure: Rethinking Assessment Through the Arts*. New York: College Entrance Examination Board, 1991.

Yenawine, Philip. *Key Art Terms for Beginners*. New York: Harry N. Abrams, Inc., 1995.

———. *Colors*. New York: Delacorte Press, 1991.

———. *Lines*. New York: Delacorte Press, 1991.

———. *Shapes*. New York: Delacorte Press, 1991.

———. *Stories*. New York: Delacorte Press, 1991.

Zakkai, Jennifer Donohue. *Dance as a Way of Knowing*. Strategies for Teaching and Learning Professional Library series, The Galef Institute. York, Maine: Stenhouse Publishers, 1997.

Zhensun, Zheng and Alice Low. *A Young Painter: The Life and Paintings of Wang Yani—China's Extraordinary Young Artist*. New York: Scholastic, 1991.

Children's Bibliography

Arnold, Tedd. *The Signmaker's Assistant*. New York: Dial Books, 1992. A mischievous signmaker's apprentice wreaks havoc on his town by posting his own silly and confusing signs all over his community, but learns to appreciate the importance of his craft and accept responsibility for his actions.

Arnosky, Jim. *Near the Sea*. New York: Lothrop, Lee and Shepard, 1990. Vivid oil paintings capture the glorious seashores and saltwater marshes as well as the abundant wildlife on a small island off the coast of Maine.

Baylor, Byrd. *I'm in Charge of Celebrations*. Illustrated by Peter Parnall. New York: Scribner's, 1986. A woman finds beauty and meaning in the natural events that surround her home in the desert by creating poetic celebrations of seemingly ordinary happenings.

_____. *When Clay Sings*. Illustrated by Tom Bahti. New York: Aladdin, Macmillan, 1972. The ancient designs on prehistoric Indian pottery from the southwestern desert region of what is now the United States reveal customs and traditions of early life.

Beatty, Patricia. *O the Red Rose Tree*. Illustrated by Liz Dauber. New York: Morrow Junior Books, 1994. Four friends join an elderly woman in an adventure and search for seven different shades of red fabric to complete her unique quilt.

Berger, Barbara Helen. *Grandfather Twilight*. New York: Philomel Books, 1984. A beautifully written and illustrated story about old Grandfather

Twilight, who walks through the woods and brings on twilight and the closely following night.

Björk, Christina. *Linnea in Monet's Garden*. Illustrated by Lena Anderson. New York: Farrar, Straus and Giroux, 1987. Linnea, a young girl, visits the famous home and garden of Claude Monet in Giverney, France, and satisfies her curiosity about the artist and the Impressionist painters.

Bolton, Jane. *My Grandmother's Patchwork Quilt*. New York: Doubleday, 1994. A delightful family story told through a magnificent quilt. Instructions and ten fabrics pieces provide help to get started on making a patchwork quilt.

Brown, Marcia. *Shadow*. New York: Scribner's, 1982. Stunning collages, bold usage of vibrant colors, and lyrical text tell the story of Shadow, a mysterious figure from African folklore.

Capek, Michael. *Artistic Trickery: The Tradition of Trompe L'Oeil Art*. Minneapolis, Minnesota: Lerner, 1995. An informative history about the art of trompe l'oeil features many examples of the art form, from ancient Greece to modern examples, exploring specific artists and common visual themes.

Carle, Eric. *Eric Carle's Animals Animals*. New York: Philomel Books, 1989. Vibrant and colorful collage illustrations accompany over fifty poems about animals from many different cultures by poets ranging from Shakespeare to Rudyard Kipling.

_____. *Draw Me a Star*. New York: Philomel Books, 1992. In Carle's distinctive and engaging illustrations, a young artist experiences the process of creation by envisioning possibilities. He creates a world by drawing a star, a sun, a tree, until he has filled up a blank white background with a world alive with color and light.

Cherry, Lynne. *A River Ran Wild*. San Diego, California: Harcourt Brace & Company, 1992. A beautifully illustrated true story of dedicated environmentalists and volunteers who save the Nashua River Valley in Massachusetts from pollution.

Chief Seattle. *Brother Eagle, Sister Sky: A Message from Chief Seattle*. Illustrated by Susan Jeffers. New York: Dial Books, 1991. A wonderfully rendered adaptation of Chief Seattle's famous 1850's speech in which he eloquently describes the central belief of Native American people: The earth and every living creature on it is sacred.

Clément, Claude. *The Painter and the Wild Swans*. Illustrated by Frédéric Clément. New York: Dial Books, 1986. This story follows the journey of a Japanese master artist as he abandons all that he has to follow a flock of magnificent wild swans in order to experience the power of their beauty.

Collins, Pat Lowery. *I Am an Artist*. Illustrated by Robin Brickman. Brookfield, Connecticut: Millbrook Press, 1992. The narrator of this superbly illustrated and imaginative book reveals that we are all artists when we stop to observe and appreciate the wonder and beauty of the nature that surrounds us.

Cummings, Pat, ed. *Talking With Artists*. New York: Bradbury Press, 1992. All children have questions they want to ask artists, such as: Where do you get ideas? Who influenced you? How do you draw those great pictures? In this book, children have a chance to learn about their favorite book illustrators who are sometimes their first connection to art and artists.

Davidson, Rosemary. *Take a Look: An Introduction to the Experience of Art*. New York: Viking, 1994. This book guides children to look, see, think, make, discover, and enjoy art as a personal and everyday experience rather than something out of the ordinary. The text is illustrated with more than two hundred reproductions, drawings, and photographs.

de Mejo, Oscar. *Oscar de Mejo's ABC*. New York: HarperCollins, 1992. In an homage to America, the artist's adopted country, this alphabet book is filled with surrealistic renderings of American history and folk art that correspond to the letters of the alphabet.

de Paola, Tomie. *Bonjour, Mr. Satie*. New York: Putnam, 1991. Mr. Satie, a well-traveled cat, invites readers to become acquainted with artists and authors like Pablo Picasso and Gertrude Stein in a story about the Parisian art community of the 1920s.

_____. *The Art Lesson*. New York: Putnam, 1989. Tommy, a young aspiring artist, learns to follow the rules of his art class, yet at the same time freely explores his own creativity within the structure of his class.

_____. *The Legend of the Indian Paintbrush*. New York: Putnam, 1988. In retelling the tale of how the Indian Paintbrush flower got it's name, readers get a glimpse of Native American culture and begin to understand the struggles faced by a young man trying to find his place in the community.

Edwards, Michelle. *A Baker's Portrait*. New York: Lothrop, Lee and Shepard, 1991. When a young painter is called upon to paint a portrait of her aunt and uncle who are bakers, she finds a way to paint her subjects realistically and honestly, yet at the same time shows their kindness and integrity.

Feelings, Tom. *Soul Looks Back in Wonder*. New York: Dial Books, 1993. Older readers can celebrate the African American experience and it's creative force in poems by Maya Angelou, Langston Hughes, and many other poets whose words are paired with images completed in a variety of artistic mediums.

Fennimore, Flora. *The Art of the Handmade Book*. Chicago: Chicago Review Press, 1992. The author traces the history of bookmaking from the advent of papyrus to today's mass production, and teaches children step-by-step how to bind their own books using simple, decorative techniques.

Florian, Douglas. *A Painter*. New York: Greenwillow Books, 1993. With simple text and colorful artwork, the author tells us how an artist finds his inspiration and invites children to explore the artist's tools and techniques.

Gardner, Jane Mylum. *Henry Moore: From Bones and Stones to Sketches and Sculptures:* New York: Four Winds Press, 1993. A thorough look at the British sculptor's creative process as he elevates ordinary objects, such as bones and stones, to artistic levels, by sketching, casting, and transforming these objects into monumental sculptures.

Garza, Carmen Lomas. *Family Pictures (Cuadros de Familia)*. San Francisco: Children's Book Press, 1990. The artist and author brings her childhood memories of growing up in a Hispanic community in Texas to life with vivid pictures using English and Spanish text.

Gelber, Carol. *Masks Tell Stories*. Brookfield, Connecticut: Millbrook Press, 1993. Here is a chance to learn about masks as works of art and as objects that hold a significant cultural purpose in religious ceremonies, cultural and artistic events, and occupational protection.

George, Jean Craighead. *The First Thanksgiving*. Illustrated by Thomas Locker. New York: Philomel Books, 1993. Colorful paintings bring to life the story of the Pilgrims' journey to the New World. Detailed descriptions illustrate how Squanto taught the English people necessary survival techniques, and points to the key role that Native Americans played in the history of our nation.

Glubok, Shirley. *The Art of the Northwest Coast Indians*. New York: Macmillan, 1975. With numerous photographs and easy text, this book will help acquaint students with the art of the Haida and other similar tribes.

Goble, Paul. *The Girl Who Loved Wild Horses*. New York: Aladdin, Macmillan, 1986. This Caldecott award winner tells the story of a Native American girl who gets lost as she is caught up in a stampede of wild horses during a storm. She decides to live among the creatures that she has come to love and admire rather than return home to her village.

Guback, Georgia. *Luka's Quilt*. New York: Greenwillow Books, 1994. Luka cannot hide her disappointment when the quilt her grandmother makes her is a traditional two colored Hawaiian one, instead of the multi-colored, bright quilt she was expecting. They eventually find a compromise between youthful wishes and traditional artistic principles.

Hamilton, Virginia. *The People Could Fly: American Black Folktales*. Illustrated by Leo and Diane Dillon. New York: Knopf, 1985. An excellent collection of African-American folktales finds its roots in the stories slaves told each other to express their frustrations, keep hold of their cultures, and explain the world around them.

Hopkinson, Deborah. *Sweet Clara and the Freedom Quilt.* Illustrated by James Ransome. New York: Knopf, 1993. Enchanting illustrations tell the story of a young slave girl's dreams of following the Underground Railroad to freedom and how it leads her to sew a quilt that is a map to a secret escape route north to Canada.

Hort, Lenny. *The Boy Who Held Back the Sea.* Illustrated by Thomas Locker. New York: Dial Books, 1987. A magnificently illustrated tale of a young boy who saves his town by heroically blocking a leak in the dike.

Hoyt-Goldsmith, Diane. *Totem Pole.* Photographs by Lawrence Migdale. New York: Holiday House, 1990. A unique look at modern-day tribal membership in the Eagle Clan Indian Tribe is revealed as a young boy recalls a classic folktale that helps him understand traditional Indian ceremonial rituals.

Isaacson, Phil M. *Round Buildings, Square Buildings and Buildings That Wiggle Like a Fish.* New York: Knopf, 1988. Students will have fun examining and exploring walls, materials, doorways, ornamentation, and other architectural elements that give churches, homes, lighthouses, and other buildings their unique style.

Johnson, Crockett. *Harold and the Purple Crayon.* New York: HarperCollins, 1981. The classic story about a little boy who decides to go for a walk in the moonlight. Harold takes along his giant purple crayon to create beautiful landscapes and a thrilling adventure.

Johnston, Tony. *The Quilt Story.* Illustrated by Tomie de Paola. New York: Putnam, 1985. A young girl discovers an old quilt in the attic of her house that once belonged to a little girl much like herself. Both children find comfort across the ages, in the warmth and security of the quilt.

Knight, Margy Burns. *Talking Walls.* Illustrated by Anne Sibley O'Brien. Gardiner, Maine: Tilbury House, 1992. From the Great Wall of China to the West wall in Jerusalem to the Taos Pueblos in New Mexico, this book tells about the history of the people who built these walls and decorated them.

Lawrence, Jacob. *The Great Migration.* New York: HarperCollins, 1993. A complete collection of the 60 panels from artist Jacob Lawrence's Migration Series, dramatically documents the story of one of the greatest population shifts in the history of the United States as African Americans left the south and moved north in search of work and a better life.

Lehrman, Fredric. *Loving The Earth: A Sacred Landscape Book for Children.* Illustrated by Lisa Tune. Berkeley, California: Celestial Arts, 1990. Vibrant illustrations, photographs, and simple, warm text invite children to discover the mysteries and gifts of planet Earth in order to understand why we need to cherish our planet.

Leslie, Clare Walker. *Nature All Year Long*. New York: Greenwillow Books, 1991. A wonderfully illustrated guide for burgeoning naturalists that describes the wide variety of plant life and animals that can be found each and every month.

Levine, Arthur A. *The Boy Who Drew Cats*. Illustrated by Frédéric Clément. New York: Dial Books, 1993. A Japanese folktale recounts how Kenji's family thinks his love for drawing cats is a waste of time, until one day his beautiful drawings come to life to help rid a village of a monstrous Goblin Rat.

Lionni, Leo. *Little Blue and Little Yellow*. New York: Mulberry Books, 1994. A story of the friendship between two colors, little Blue and little Yellow, that blend when they hug to become a brand new color, green.

Livingston, Myra Cohn. *Earth Songs*. Illustrated by Leonard Everett Fisher. New York: Holiday House, 1986. Livingston uses lyrical words and beautiful color illustrations to pay tribute to the earth, its continents, hills, forests, seas, and more in a book of inspirational poems.

Lobel, Arnold. *The Great Blueness and Other Predicaments*. New York: Harper & Row, 1968. A wizard finally creates color and paints his previously gray world entirely in a deep blue, then a bright yellow, and finally a blazing red. Each color is more overwhelming than the next, until he learns to mix the three original colors to paint a world all colors of the rainbow.

Locker, Thomas. *The Young Artist*. New York: Dial Books, 1989. A young apprentice to a master artist is asked to paint portraits of the members of the king's court who all want to be depicted in a positive light. The apprentice must decide whether to respond to their wishes, or maintain his sense of artistic integrity.

_____. *Where the River Begins*. New York: Dial Books, 1984. Wonderfully dramatic landscape paintings vividly illustrate this adventure in nature as two young boys go on a camping trip with their grandfather to discover the source of a river.

Lyons, Mary E. *Deep Blues: Bill Traylor, Self-Taught Artist*. New York: Scribner's, 1994. A biography about former slave and self-taught artist, Bill Traylor, who began painting and drawing on his eightieth birthday.

MacClintock, Dorcas. *Animals Observed: A Look at Animals in Art*. New York: Scribner's, 1993. An in-depth exploration of animals in paintings, sculpture, collage and other mediums rendered by artists throughout time.

Madison, Jon. *Beautiful Junk: A Story of the Watts Towers*. Photos by Barbara and Lou Jacobs Jr. Boston: Little, Brown & Company, 1968. A story about a boy who spends his day among junk, not realizing it's value, until he meets a man who helps him to see its beauty in the Watts Towers.

Marshak, Suzanna. *I Am the Ocean*. Illustrations by James Endicott. New York: Arcade Publishing, 1991. Beautiful illustrations accompany the poetic narrative as the author takes a look at the wonders, strengths, and mysteries of the ocean.

Mason, Antony. *Famous Artists: Picasso*. Hauppauge, New York: Barron's Educational Series, 1995. This is part of a series that appeals to older students as it provides an introduction to the celebrated painter and sculptor and his achievements. Hands-on projects invite readers to explore the artist's style of working. Other titles in the series include: Leonardo Da Vinci, Michelangelo, Van Gogh, Monet, and Cezanne.

McDermott, Gerald. *Arrow to the Sun*. New York: Viking, 1974. Vibrant color illustrations accompany the adaptation of a Pueblo Indian folktale that tells a tale of a boy's search for his father and how it leads him to bring the Lord of the Sun back to earth.

McLerran, Alice. *The Mountain That Loved a Bird*. Illustrated by Eric Carle. New York: Simon and Schuster, 1985. A touching story depicts the transformation of a barren mountain into a flourishing source of life for animals and plants.

Melville, Herman. *Catskill Eagle*. Illustrated by Thomas Locker. New York: Philomel Books, 1991. Using a short excerpt from Moby Dick, Thomas Locker captures the majesty of the Catskill Mountains in upstate New York. Readers will glimpse the gorges, forests, and peaks of the mountain from an eagle's point of view—one of soaring heights.

Micklethwait, Lucy. *A Child's Book of Art: Great Pictures, First Words*. New York: Dorling Kindersley, 1993. Over 100 different works of art by artists as diverse as Michelangelo and David Hockney introduce young readers to the world of art appreciation.

Monceaux, Morgan. *Jazz: My Music, My People*. New York: Knopf, 1994. An African American artist pays tribute to the jazz greats of our time by providing older readers with impressionistic vignettes, biographical sketches, and striking color illustrations.

Munthe, Nelly. *Meet Matisse*. Boston: Little, Brown & Company, 1983. A large selection of Henri Matisse's bold cutouts as well as instructions for mixing colors, creating textures in paint, and composing Matisse-like works, introduce children to the art of collage.

Neimark, Anne E. *Diego Rivera: Artist of the People*. New York: HarperCollins, 1992. A fictionalized biography of the famous Mexican muralist discusses some of the artist's most important and monumental murals about the everyday lives of the common man, as well as Rivera's artistic technique and the impact of his work.

Oram, Hiawyn. *Out of the Blue: Poems About Color*. Illustrated by David McKee. New York: Hyperion Books, 1993. A collection of whimsical poems all about colors that are paired with accompanying illustrations.

Paul, Anne Whitford. *Eight Hands Round: A Patchwork Alphabet.* Illustrated by Jeanette Winter. New York: HarperCollins, 1991. The origins of quilt designs are examined in the context of American history in this beautifully illustrated book.

Polacco, Patricia. *The Keeping Quilt.* New York: Simon and Schuster, 1998. After immigrating to America from Russia, a Jewish family sews a quilt from the family's old clothes to remind them of home. The quilt is passed from mother to daughter for over a century. It's used as a wedding canopy, a Sabbath tablecloth, and a blanket that welcomes babies into the world.

Potter, Beatrix. *The Tale of Peter Rabbit.* London, England: Penguin, 1993. The classic tale about a mischievous rabbit named Peter who gets into trouble when he ventures into Mr. McGregor's garden.

Raboff, Ernest. *Art for Children* series. New York: Harper & Row, 1988. Raboff's series provides an accessible introduction to some of the world's greatest artists. Each book in this series contains a biography, an interpretation of the artist's work, as well as full-color reproductions. The artists featured in this series include: Matisse, Renoir, Raphael, Gauguin, Klee, Rousseau, Chagall, Rembrandt, Da Vinci, Picasso, Michelangelo, Velazquez, Rousseau, Remington, Dürer, and Toulouse-Lautrec.

Radin, Ruth Yaffe. *High in the Mountains.* Illustrated by Ed Young. New York: Macmillan, 1989. A story-poem about a young child who spends a day in the mountains amid the wildflowers, deer, and afternoon shadows. Filled with whimsical watercolor illustrations by Ed Young, it offers students a rich view of mountain life.

Richardson, Wendy and Jack. *The World of Art* series. Chicago, Illinois: Childrens Press, 1991. As the authors put it, we can "explore the world through the eyes of artists and see how people from many different countries have expressed their understanding, feelings, and thoughts through art." The books are theme-based collection of images and artwork for teachers and children. The titles in this series include: *Animals, Families, Cities, Entertainers, The Natural World,* and *Water.*

Richmond, Robin. *Introducing Michelangelo.* Boston: Little, Brown & Company, 1992. A thorough look at the life and times of Michelangelo, as students learn to appreciate his sculptures and paintings within the historical context of the Renaissance.

Ringgold, Faith. *Aunt Harriet's Underground Railroad in the Sky.* New York: Crown, 1992. Cassie Louise Lightfoot, the heroine of Tar Beach, embarks on a wondrous, dream-like journey as she and her guide Harriet Tubman, fly through the sky, chasing the train her little brother has boarded, on its way north to freedom.

_____. *Dinner at Aunt Connie's House*. New York: Hyperion Books, 1993. Nine-year-old Melody and her new friend Lonnie come across paintings of famous African American women in the attic. Each woman in the painting tells of her unique and courageous contribution to history.

Roalf, Peggy. *Dancers. Looking at Paintings* series. New York: Hyperion Books, 1992. Students become familiar with the history of dance and dancers by viewing various images of dance by artists such as Degas, Blake, Toulouse-Lautrec, and many others. Roalf's other titles include *Children, Horses, Landscapes*, and *Self-Portraits*, among others. The reader is taken on a visual tour of many different painters' views of a single subject.

Robertson, Kayo. *Signs Along the River: Learning To Read the Natural Landscape*. Boulder, Colorado: Roberts Rinehart Inc., 1986. Detailed line drawings by Roberston and gentle words guide students to track the wildlife along a riverbed. Students learn to "read" natural signs such as footprints, ripples in water, and chewed grass.

Say, Allen. *Grandfather's Journey*. Boston: Houghton Mifflin, 1993. This beautifully illustrated tale helps children understand the emotions of leaving one's homeland to explore a new country. Allan Say tells the story of his grandfather's journey from Japan to America, and the longing he felt to be in both places at once.

Scott, Elaine. *Funny Papers: Behind the Scenes of the Comics*. Photos by Margaret Miller. New York: Morrow Junior Books, 1993. A delightful look at the history of comics and how they are conceived, drawn, syndicated, published, and printed. The author also examines the social and historical significance of comics through the study of old political cartoons as well as popular cartoons of our day.

Sills, Leslie. *Inspirations: Stories About Women Artists*. Niles, Illinois: Albert Whitman, 1989. A fascinating introduction to the works and lives of four famous contemporary women artists: Frida Kahlo, Faith Ringgold, Georgia O'Keeffe, and Alice Neel.

Staines, Bill. *River*. Illustrated by Kate Spohn. New York: Viking, 1994. Beautiful, impressionistic paintings illustrate and accompany a folk singer's lyrical musings on the ever changing river, a source of constant inspiration to the writer.

Stockham, Peter. *Early American Crafts and Trades*. New York: Dover Publications, 1976. This lovely little book, a reprint of a volume from 1807, describes twenty-three early American trades in intricate detail and contains great copperplate engravings.

Sturgis, Alexander. *Introducing Rembrandt*. Boston: Little, Brown & Company, 1994. Rembrandt's drawings, prints, paintings, and contributions to the Western artistic tradition are explored in this full-colored book.

Sufrin, Mark. *George Catlin: Painter of the Indian West*. New York: Atheneum, 1991. A complete biographical look at the artist's fascination with painting and studying aspects of Indian life.

Swentzell, Rina. *Children of Clay: A Family of Pueblo Potters*. Minneapolis, Minnesota: Lerner, 1992. This book takes a photographic look at a Tewa family's age-old tradition of clay making. The book follows them from finding the clay to the creation of pottery and figures.

Turner, Robyn Montana. *Rosa Bonheur. Portraits of Women Artists for Children* series. Boston: Little, Brown & Company, 1991. A biography of the famous painter who was known for her realistic, yet heroic and dramatic paintings of animals in the late 1800s. The series examines the problems and obstacles faced by many female artists of the day. Other titles in the series feature artists Mary Cassatt, Frida Kahlo, Georgia O'Keeffe, and Faith Ringgold.

Van Allsburg, Chris. *Just a Dream*. Boston: Houghton Mifflin, 1990. After a dream makes a little boy aware of what might happen if he doesn't take care of his surroundings, he reconsiders how he treats the environment.

Venezia, Mike. *Picasso. Getting To Know the World's Greatest Artists* series. Chicago: Children's Press, 1988. Venezia provides an enjoyable look at the life and works of Pablo Picasso in a guided tour through different periods of the artist's development. Whimsical cartoon illustrations and full color reproductions make the book accessible to young children. Other artists featured in this series include Van Gogh, Goya, Hopper, Botticelli, Klee, Da Vinci, Michelangelo, Rembrandt, Cassatt, and Monet.

Walker, Lou Ann. *Roy Lichtenstein: The Artist at Work*. Photos by Michael Abramson. New York: Lodestar Books, 1994. Remarkable color photographs of Lichtenstein's artworks create a photo-essay of the artist's creative process and his work.

Wells, Rosemary. *Night Sounds, Morning Colors*. Illustrated by David McPhail. New York: Dial Books, 1994. A young boy uses his senses to ponder the wonders of sunlight that comes pouring in through the window. The smell of old leather and the pine forest among other things are described in prose and illustrated in atmospheric renderings.

Welton, Jude. *Drawing: A Young Artist's Guide*. New York: Dorling Kindersley, 1994. Young artists learn practical techniques to create light, shade, pattern, and texture using pencils, charcoals, and paints. Included are examples from the Tate Gallery in London.

Willard, Nancy. *Pish, Posh, Said Hieronymus Bosch*. Illustrated by Leo and Diane Dillon. San Diego, California: Harcourt Brace Jovanovich, 1991. An opulent book about a housekeeper who works for the medieval Dutch artist Hieronymus Bosch. His menagerie of bizarre creatures and beasts come to life in his paintings only to create havoc in the household.

_____. *The Nightgown of the Sullen Moon*. Illustrated by David McPhail. San Diego, California: Harcourt Brace Jovanovich, 1983. In this enchanting story, children are invited to engage in a bit of fantasy about the Moon and what it wants. Subtle watercolors by David McPhail create just the right environment for the reader's adventures with the moon.

Winter, Jeanette. *Follow the Drinking Gourd*. New York: Knopf, 1988. This is the story of one family's journey from slavery to freedom along the Underground Railroad. Told in a picture-book format, the story is a good springboard for a discussion of slavery and the events that led to the Civil War.

Winter, Jonah. *Diego*. Illustrated by Jeanette Winter. New York: Knopf, 1991. A simple look at the life of Diego Rivera as a young child and struggling artist in both English and Spanish, where the illustrations are done in an homage to Rivera's epic style.

Yarbrough, Camille. *Cornrows*. Illustrated by Carole Byard. New York: Coward McCann, Inc., 1979. Written from the perspective of a young African American girl, this story explains how the hairstyle of braid, or cornrows, can symbolize the courage of outstanding African Americans. Much of the text is written in rhyming verse with illustrations of black and white paintings by Carole Byard.

Yenawine, Philip. *Lines*. New York: Delacorte Press, 1991. In a series of books on modern art, Yenawine helps young children explore the basic vocabulary of artists by guiding thoughtful looking at the work of well-known artists. Books about *People, Places, Shapes, Colors and Stories* complete the series.

Yolen, Jane. *Owl Moon*. Illustrated by John Schoenherr. New York: Philomel Books, 1987. In this Caldecott-winning book, a father and daughter trek into the woods with the hope of sighting an elusive owl. Watercolor illustrations by John Schoenherr and sensory language combine to bring this winter forest night to life.

Zheng, Zhensun and Alice Low. *A Young Painter: The life and paintings of Wang Yani—China's extraordinary young artist*. New York: Scholastic Inc., 1991. The amazing story of youthful Chinese painter Wang Yani will inspire aspiring artists. All will be enchanted with her impressive paintings of monkeys, peacocks, and the rural landscapes. Full color reproductions and photographs of Wang Yani's paintings capture the excitement she has generated in her world-wide exhibitions.

Professional Associations and Publications

The American Alliance for Health,
Physical Education,
Recreation, and Dance (AAHPERD)
*Journal of Physical Education, Recreation,
and Dance*
1900 Association Drive
Reston, Virginia 22091

American Alliance for Theater and Education
(AATE)
AATE Newsletter
c/o Arizona State University Theater
Department
Box 873411
Tempe, Arizona 85287

American Association for the Advancement
of Science (AAAS)
Science Magazine
1333 H Street NW
Washington, DC 20005

American Association of Colleges for Teacher
Education (AACTE)
AACTE Briefs
1 DuPont Circle NW, Suite 610
Washington, DC 20036

American Association of School
Administrators (AASA)
The School Administrator
1801 North Moore Street
Arlington, Virginia 22209

Arts Education Partnership
Council of Chief State School Officers
One Massachusetts Avenue, NW, Suite 700
Washington, DC 20001-1431

Association for Childhood Education
International (ACEI)
*Childhood Education: Infancy Through
Early Adolescence*

11141 Georgia Avenue, Suite 200
Wheaton, Maryland 20902

American Music Conferernce (AMC)
5790 Armada Drive
Carlsbad, CA 92008

Association for Supervision and Curriculum
Development (ASCD)
Educational Leadership
1250 North Pitt Street
Alexandria, Virginia 22314

The Council for Exceptional Children (CEC)
Teaching Exceptional Children
1920 Association Drive
Reston, Virginia 22091

Education Theater Association (ETA)
Dramatics
3368 Central Parkway
Cincinnati, Ohio 45225

J. Paul Getty Museum
Department for Education in the Arts
1200 Getty Center Drive
Los Angeles, California 90049-1681

International Reading Association (IRA)
The Reading Teacher
800 Barksdale Road
Newark, Delaware 19714

The John F. Kennedy Center for the
Performing Arts
Washington, D.C. 20566

The Mid-South California Arts Project Open
Institute at California State University
Northridge; TSMCAP is a regional site of The
California
Arts Project

Music Educators National Conference (MENC)
Music Educators Journal
1806 Robert Fulton Drive
Reston, Virginia 22091

National Art Education Association (NAEA)
Art Education
1916 Association Drive
Reston, Virginia 22091

National Association for the Education of
Young Children (NAEYC)
Young Children
1509 16th Street NW
Washington, DC 20036

National Association of Elementary School
Principals (NAESP)
Communicator
1615 Duke Street
Alexandria, Virginia 22314

National Center for Restructuring Education,
Schools, and Teaching (NCREST)
Resources for Restructuring
P.O. Box 110
Teachers College, Columbia University
New York, New York 10027

National Council for the Social Studies (NCSS)
Social Education
Social Studies and the Young Learner
3501 Newark Street, NW
Washington, DC 20016

National Council of Supervisors of
Mathematics (NCSM)
*NCSM Newsletter Leadership in Mathematics
Education*
P.O. Box 10667
Golden, Colorado 80401

National Council of Teachers of English
(NCTE)
Language Arts
Primary Voices K-6
1111 Kenyon Road
Urbana, Illinois 61801

National Council of Teachers of Mathematics (NCTM)
Arithmetic Teacher
Teaching Children Mathematics
1906 Association Drive
Reston, Virginia 22091

National Dance Association (NDA)
Spotlight on Dance
1900 Association Drive
Reston, Virginia 22091

National Science Teachers Association (NSTA)
Science and Children
Science for Children: Resources for Teachers
1840 Wilson Boulevard
Arlington, Virginia 22201

Phi Delta Kappa
Phi Delta Kappan
408 North Union
Bloomington, Indiana 47402

Smithsonian Institution
100 Jefferson Drive SW
Washington, DC 20560

Society for Research in Music Education
Journal for Research in Music Education
c/o Music Educators National Conference
1806 Robert Fulton Drive
Reston, Virginia 22091

The Southern Poverty Law Center
Teaching Tolerance
400 Washington Avenue
Montgomery, Alabama 36104

Teachers of English to Speakers of Other Languages (TESOL)
TESOL Newsletter
1600 Cameron Street, Suite 300
Alexandria, Virginia 22314